THE LIGHTS

BY HOWARD KORDER

★

★

DRAMATISTS
PLAY SERVICE
INC.

In memory of my father,
who knew the fields of Inwood

all I want is a room up there
and you in it
— Frank O'Hara

THE LIGHTS received its premiere at the Lincoln Center Theater (André Bishop, Artistic Director; Bernard Gersten, Executive Producer) in New York City, on November 3, 1993. It was directed by Mark Wing-Davey; the set design was by Marina Draghici; the costume design was by Laura Cunningham; the lighting design was by Christopher Akerlind and additional music and sound were by Mark Bennett. The cast was as follows:

ROSE .... Kristen Johnston
LILLIAN .... Kathleen Dennehy
CUSTOMER, WOMAN WITH JUNK,
    SPECTATOR ONE .... Ileen Getz
MAN IN OVERCOAT, MAN ONE, MAN WITH
    CUP, MANAGER, SCAB TWO .... Steven Goldstein
KRAUS, SPECTATOR FOUR .... Todd Weeks
FREDRIC .... Dan Futterman
MAN IN CHAIR, SCAB THREE .... Leon Addison Brown
MAN TWO, SPECTATOR THREE,
    BILL, GUARD, SCAB ONE .... David Pittu
SPEAKER, MAN WITH PANTS .... Ray Anthony Thomas
SPECTATOR TWO, WAITER TWO,
    MR. BARRY .... Jordan Lage
SPECTATOR FIVE, ERENHART .... Christopher McCann
MAN WITH CAMERA .... Andrew Mutnick
WAITER ONE, ART .... Herbert Rubens
YOUNG WAITER, FOREMAN .... Neil Pepe
DIAMOND .... Jerry Grayson
PASSERSBY .... Tom Bloom, Robin Spielberg

THE LIGHTS was presented by the Atlantic Theater Company (Neil Pepe, Artistic Director), in Burlington, Vermont, in August, 1993, as a workshop production. It was directed by Mark Wing-Davey.

THE LIGHTS was originally commissioned by South Coast Repertory Theater, Costa Mesa, California.

CHARACTERS

LILIAN, 20s
FREDRIC, 20s
ROSE, 20s
ERENHART, early 40s
DIAMOND, 50s
CUSTOMER
MAN IN OVERCOAT
KRAUS
STRANGER (ART)
MAN IN CHAIR
MAN ONE
MAN TWO
WOMAN WITH JUNK
SPEAKER
SPECTATOR ONE
SPECTATOR TWO
SPECTATOR THREE

SPECTATOR FOUR
SPECTATOR FIVE
MAN WITH CAMERA
WAITER ONE
WAITER TWO
MANAGER
YOUNG WAITER
BILL
MAN WITH PANTS
GUARD
MR. BARRY
SCAB ONE
SCAB TWO
SCAB THREE
FOREMAN
PASSERBYS

PLACE

A large city.

TIME

The modern era.

THE LIGHTS

SCENE ONE

Department store counter. Lilian, Rose. Three tones sound.

ROSE.   In the city?

LILIAN.   Mmm.

ROSE.   Somebody opens a door every half-second. *(Pause. Lilian yawns.)*

LILIAN.   Huh?

ROSE.   What?

LILIAN.   Who's opening the door all the time.

ROSE.   You're not listening.

LILIAN.   Sure I am.

ROSE.   What did I say.

LILIAN.   Some guy is always opening a door.

ROSE.   No. In the *city*. They did a *study*.

LILIAN.   Oh.

ROSE.   There are so many people that every half a second somewhere —

LILIAN.   I get it.

ROSE.   I mean if you think of it it's, it's ... *(Pause.)* It's too much to even imagine. *(Silence.)*

LILIAN.   Three doors.

ROSE.   Huh?

LILIAN.   Just now. *(Rose looks at her blankly.)* Nothing. *(Pause.)*

ROSE.   Twenty-seven minutes. *(Customer enters.)* Hello, welcome to Tuckman's. May I help you?

CUSTOMER.   I'm only looking.

ROSE.   Everything with a yellow tag is fifteen percent off today.

CUSTOMER.   Uh-hmm. *(They watch her browse.)*

LILIAN.   Let us know if we can help you.

CUSTOMER.   How much is that watch?

LILIAN.   Twenty-three ninety-five.

CUSTOMER.   Uh-hmm.

LILIAN.   It's the most popular men's style. *(Customer examines watch.)* You can put it on layaway ...

CUSTOMER.   Are you going out of business?

LILIAN.   Excuse me?

CUSTOMER.   I heard you were going out of business.

LILIAN.   No ...

CUSTOMER.   I don't want to buy something and see it marked down again.

LILIAN.   We're not going anywhere.

CUSTOMER.   And I could have gotten it half-price. *(Customer looks at watch, then lays it on counter.)* I'll wait.

LILIAN.   Sale's only this week. *(Customer exits.)*

ROSE.   Thank you for shopping at Tuckman's! *(Pause.)* Some people?

LILIAN.   Hmm.

ROSE.   You look at their faces you see how they'll be when they're *old. (Pause.)*

LILIAN.   Is the store going to close?

ROSE.   I don't know.

LILIAN.   Have you heard something?

ROSE.   Nobody's talking.

LILIAN.   I don't want to lose my job.

ROSE.   No kidding.

LILIAN.   My boyfriend's looking for a job and he can't find anything.

ROSE.   You still with him?

LILIAN.   I guess so. Yeah I am. *(Pause.)*

ROSE.   *I* have a date.

LILIAN.   Who?

ROSE.   This guy. He asked me out. We're seeing a show.

LILIAN.   Which?

ROSE.   *Happy Go Lucky.*

LILIAN.   That's supposed to be good.

ROSE.   I know.

LILIAN. How'd you get seats?

ROSE. He's very well connected. People give him things for free.

LILIAN. Could he get me in?

ROSE. Well … I'll *ask*. *(Pause. Looking off.)* Here comes your sweetheart.

LILIAN. Huh? *(Following Rose's gaze.)* Very funny.

ROSE. Look at the gloves. The gloves are new.

LILIAN. Why's he keep coming in here.

ROSE. He's in *love* with you.

LILIAN. Stop it. *(Man in worn overcoat, wearing gloves, comes up to counter.)* Yes?

MAN IN OVERCOAT. I want to buy … the cykapedia.

LILIAN. We don't have that.

MAN IN OVERCOAT. There's things I'm supposed to read today.

LILIAN. We don't carry encyclopedias.

MAN IN OVERCOAT. It's got my face, I need it back.

ROSE. You're not allowed in the store.

MAN IN OVERCOAT. They hid my face in the cykapedia …

ROSE. You hear me?

MAN IN OVERCOAT. Which they can't, it's against the law …

ROSE. Remember last time? Hmm? We'll call the guard.

MAN IN OVERCOAT. *Where did you put my face?*

ROSE. We'll call him, I'm calling him now. *(Pause. Man turns and leaves.)* That's right, go on … *(They watch him go.)* That was charming. I really needed *that* to happen.

LILIAN. Why don't they stop him at the *door*.

ROSE. You could bring a rhino on a leash, they wouldn't notice.

LILIAN. He looked worse.

ROSE. Than who.

LILIAN. The other time.

ROSE. Well. Too bad. *(Pause.)* Gonna sneak a cigarette.

LILIAN. Mmm-hmm. *(Rose exits. Lilian stands there. She picks up watch from counter. To herself.)* Why not. *(She slips it in her pocket. She looks around quickly. Kraus walks by with white flower in his lapel.)*

KRAUS. Everything copacetic here?
LILIAN. Yes, Mr. Kraus. *(Pause.)*
KRAUS. *(Remembering.)* "Lilian."
LILIAN. That's me.
KRAUS. Good. Very good. *(Pause.)* No makeup today.
LILIAN. Yes, I'm wearing. It's just ... how I look.
KRAUS. Ah. *(Pause.)* All right. Busy busy. *(He exits. Three tones sound. Lilian lets out a breath.)*

SCENE TWO

Street corner. Passerbys. Frederic looking through classified ads in paper. A Stranger stands next to him.

STRANGER. Got the time?
FREDRIC. No. *(Pause.)* Sorry.
STRANGER. Okay. *(Pause.)* "Looking for a job." *(Pause.)*
FREDRIC. Yuh. *(Stranger looks at paper over Fredric's shoulder.)*
STRANGER. *(Reading)* Bookkeeper ... Budget Analyst ... Chef ... Chemist ... takes brains to be a chemist, huh ... Drivers, Be Your Own Boss, it's tough. Tough getting by these days.
FREDRIC. Well. *(He steps away.)*
STRANGER. Nah, don't go, I want to ask you something. *(Pause.)*
FREDRIC. Yes.
STRANGER. How many people in this town, seven eight million.
FREDRIC. I don't know.
STRANGER. You ever see any of 'em screwing? No. Millions a people, you never see a thing. But it happens, huh? Happening *right this second*. Everybody takes their clothes off sooner or later. *(Pause.)*
FREDRIC. Got no change, okay?
STRANGER. Not even a *quarter*?
FREDRIC. No.

10

STRANGER. But I'm *hungry*, sir. I have a *disease*. I need your *help*. Won't you *help* me please?

FREDRIC. Next time.

STRANGER. Next time? Next time? That's such bullshit.

FREDRIC. *(Moving away.)* Whatever you want. *(Stranger grabs his elbow.)*

STRANGER. You *owe* someone something.

FREDRIC. No I don't.

STRANGER. You're mean. You're a mean person. You should take a little time. You should think about the things you owe to other people.

FREDRIC. Get off — *(Stranger punches Fredric in the gut.)*

STRANGER. Think about it. *(He casually walks away. Fredric drops to his knees. Passerbys step around him.)*

SCENE THREE

Apartment building. Lilian on stoop pressing intercom button, Man sitting on sidewalk in beat-up ornate armchair.

MAN IN CHAIR. Lovely girl. *(Lilian doesn't look at him.)* Excuse me, lovely girl. I'm talking to you. Excuse me. Please. Just a minute. *(She turns to him.)*

LILIAN. Yes?

MAN IN CHAIR. I'm not a stranger. We *know* each other. *(Pause.)*

LILIAN. What do you want?

MAN IN CHAIR. I want to say hello. *(Pause.)* You seeing that boy upstairs. *(Pause.)*

LILIAN. Right.

MAN IN CHAIR. I told you. We know each other. *(Pause.)*

LILIAN. You have a little dog.

MAN IN CHAIR. There you go.

LILIAN. I didn't recognize you without the dog.

MAN IN CHAIR. He's inside today. He's not feeling well.

LILIAN. Oh. I'm sorry. I hope he, uh ...

MAN IN CHAIR. I thank you very much. *(Lilian presses button again.)*

LILIAN. Where *is* he ...

MAN IN CHAIR. Keep at it. I seen him go in. *(Lilian presses the button several times. Pause.)* Now this chair?

LILIAN. Yes?

MAN IN CHAIR. Came out the garbage.

LILIAN. Really.

MAN IN CHAIR. Nothing wrong with it. You could live on what people throw out and never spend a dime.

LILIAN. You look like a king there.

MAN IN CHAIR. I feel like one. Sitting in my chair saying hello to all my people going by. Keeping an eye on things. *(Pause. Lilian presses button again.)*

FREDRIC'S VOICE. *(Through intercom.)* Yeah.

LILIAN. *(Into speaker.)* Finally, it's me.

FREDRIC'S VOICE. Who's there?

LILIAN. Me.

FREDRIC'S VOICE. Who is it?

MAN IN CHAIR. You got to yell.

LILIAN. ME. IT'S ME. *(Pause.)* OPEN THE DOOR. *(Door lock buzzes loudly.)*

MAN IN CHAIR. In you go. Take care.

LILIAN. You too.

MAN IN CHAIR. How about a smile? Come on. *(Lilian makes herself smile.)* All right. Don't forget about us now! *(Lilian goes inside.)*

SCENE FOUR

Room. Lilian, Fredric.

LILIAN. I was buzzing forever.
FREDRIC. Couldn't hear.
LILIAN. Were you asleep?
FREDRIC. No, I just.... How's it out.
LILIAN. Sort of one thing the other.
FREDRIC. Raining?
LILIAN. No, not really. It was coolish before but now it's not. I brought you something.
FREDRIC. What.
LILIAN. You want it?
FREDRIC. Sure, what is it.
LILIAN. It was on sale at the store. Plus my discount so.... It's not wrapped, sorry. *(Pause.)* It's a watch.
FREDRIC. Yeah, hey.
LILIAN. It tells time in ten different cities. *Paris* ...
FREDRIC. Right, look at that.
LILIAN. Anyway I thought you'd like it. That's why.
FREDRIC. Sure, I lost my other one.
LILIAN. That's why I did it.
FREDRIC. I ever catch that bastard ...
LILIAN. It doesn't matter.
FREDRIC. With*out* his friends.
LILIAN. You wouldn't know him.
FREDRIC. Bet I would.
LILIAN. Well you have another one now.
FREDRIC. Yeah.
LILIAN. So it doesn't matter, right? *(Pause.)*
FREDRIC. You know what time?
LILIAN. Uh-uh.
FREDRIC. Check the cola sign.
LILIAN. Which.
FREDRIC. Out the *window. (Pause.)*
LILIAN. Two thirty-eight.

FREDRIC.   That's not right. Goddamn thing never works.
Two thirty-eight a hundred twenty degrees …
LILIAN.   There *he* is.
FREDRIC.   Who.
LILIAN.   The other apartment his underwear.
FREDRIC.   Loony old geezer.
LILIAN.   Is he barking today?
FREDRIC.   Woof woof.
LILIAN.   What does he *want*.
FREDRIC.   A biscuit.
LILIAN.   Ho ho.
FREDRIC.   A dish of water, someone to scratch his belly …
LILIAN.   What's with you?
FREDRIC.   Huh?
LILIAN.   You're all bent over.
FREDRIC.   I'm fine.
LILIAN.   Hurt yourself?
FREDRIC.   Nope. *(Pause.)* So I gotta go downtown.
LILIAN.   When?
FREDRIC.   Now, whenever, I don't know what time it is.
LILIAN.   What about dinner.
FREDRIC.   Not having dinner. *(Pause.)*
LILIAN.   I bought things. I *arranged* —
FREDRIC.   I gotta *see* this guy.
LILIAN.   Still with that …
FREDRIC.   He *owes* me *money*.
LILIAN.   Let it go.
FREDRIC.   For the *work* that I *did*.
LILIAN.   Can't you just relax.
FREDRIC.   I'm *behind*.
LILIAN.   For a minute?
FREDRIC.   I keep telling you. Sitting here like this I'm fall-
ing behind.
LILIAN.   You'll find another job.
FREDRIC.   Every second.
LILIAN.   It takes time.
FREDRIC.   And that *other* guy out hustling, I know it.
LILIAN.   What guy.

FREDRIC. That *guy*. That other *guy*.

LILIAN. Oh. You mean the guy you say "hold it" he always lets the elevator close in your face?

FREDRIC. Right.

LILIAN. Guy on the train he always takes up two seats he won't put his legs together even when you shove him?

FREDRIC. See, you know him.

LILIAN. I'm looking at him.

FREDRIC. I don't do that. You think I do that?

LILIAN. Well.

FREDRIC. That *hurts*. I always give up my seat. Old ladies, cripples, nuns, babies, I gave *you* my seat.

LILIAN. You were trying to pick me up.

FREDRIC. Okay. It *worked*.

LILIAN. "Miss, you look so sad ..."

FREDRIC. Come *on*.

LILIAN. What'd you think when you saw me.

FREDRIC. What I think? *(Pause.)* Uh ...

LILIAN. Oh, don't bother.

FREDRIC. No, wait, I was thinking ... thinking ... this beautiful girl ... this innocent girl ...

LILIAN. Mmm-hmm ...

FREDRIC. I could get her wallet like *that*.

LILIAN. How about now?

FREDRIC. What.

LILIAN. Would you give me your seat now?

FREDRIC. Geez, I'd have to.

LILIAN. That's not what I meant. *(Pause.)*

FREDRIC. People who relax ...

LILIAN. No they don't.

FREDRIC. ... get flattened by trucks, they do, read the paper.

LILIAN. I don't see any trucks in here.

FREDRIC. You don't? Oh. Well that's a load off my ... *(Fredric imitates sound of screeching brakes and throws himself on the floor. Weakly.)* Lily ... Lilian ...

LILIAN. Stop.

FREDRIC. No ... I have to ... tell you something ...

LILIAN. Yes?

FREDRIC. I'm ... relaxing. *(He "dies.")*

LILIAN. Then you won't need this. *(Lilian pretends to steal his watch. Fredric grabs her arm.)*

FREDRIC. Come downtown.

LILIAN. No.

FREDRIC. Please, we'll go to the Concourse.

LILIAN. "Pinball."

FREDRIC. Did I say any —

LILIAN. I know you. You spend hours.

FREDRIC. A game of *skill*. There's *champions*.

LILIAN. I have to *eat* something.

FREDRIC. I'll treat you to Chinese. *(Pause.)* I'm getting paid. *(Pause.)*

LILIAN. Oh put your pants on.

FREDRIC. No I'm going like this.

LILIAN. Maybe you are, you're stupid enough. *(Fredric starts dressing.)*

FREDRIC. Yeah so gonna get my *money*, pay that guy, blow off the rent one week ... taking ten outta your purse ...

LILIAN. ... Right ...

FREDRIC. ... Get the *phone* back on buy some *cigarettes* and ... what. Some goddamn thing. What did I forget ...

LILIAN. Pretty ...

FREDRIC. What.

LILIAN. The sun sets and the lights go on. The buildings stick out against the sky ...

FREDRIC. Sirens up and down the street all day. I bet someone went nuts. *(Pause.)*

LILIAN. If I go ...

FREDRIC. We'll have fun, come on.

LILIAN. You'll be in a good mood, promise.

FREDRIC. I just have to meet —

LILIAN. Do you promise.

FREDRIC. I gotta get this stuff *together*, after that everything's —

LILIAN. No. Not after. Now. We're alive *now*. *(Pause.)*

FREDRIC. I promise.

16

LILIAN.   That's all I asked. *(Pause.)*
FREDRIC.   Missed you today.
LILIAN.   Did you.
FREDRIC.   I fell asleep on the subway. I was sweating. I wasn't sure where I was. I couldn't remember where I was going. *(Pause.)* So I just thought about you. Wished you were there. *(Pause.)*
LILIAN.   The whole world's not crashing together at once, you know. There's a second at least when everybody ... stops to breathe. *(Pause.)* Okay?
FREDRIC.   Yeah. *(Pause.)*
LILIAN.   My little city boy.
FREDRIC.   That's me. *(Pause.)* You could give me a kiss. *(Lilian looks at him. Fredric steps forward. They kiss.)*

SCENE FIVE

Elevated train. Two Men holding onto straps.

MAN ONE.   I'm gonna fuck her up.
MAN TWO.   Damn straight.
MAN ONE.   Motherfucking bitch.
MAN TWO.   You know it.
MAN ONE.   Like she never knew the fucker and I seen — Where are we ...
MAN TWO.   Two more. *(Fredric and Lilian enter and stand next to the men.)*
MAN ONE.   Like she never knew and I *seen* 'em both right in the back.
MAN TWO.   At the Skyline?
MAN ONE.   That back booth.
MAN TWO.   That's fucked up shit.
MAN ONE.   She *is* fucked up. Change the fucking lock tell me I don't live there anymore. Call the fucking cops, I'm *scared.*
MAN TWO.   So what.

MAN ONE. That's right. Teach her a lesson, that bitch. I told her don't fuck with me, you fucking cunt. Sitting on the stoop —

MAN TWO. I saw him.

MAN ONE. Say don't come near me, I got protection?

MAN TWO. Fullashit.

MAN ONE. You wanna fuck with me, ask around. Shit-eating pussy faggot. You ask anyone the whole fucking city they wanna fuck with me. You don't know what you're talking with. Not some fuck-ass game, fucking city is where. You and that cocksucking cunt bitch I'll fuck you both up laughing. With the six inch blade.

MAN TWO. What he do? *(Pause.)*

MAN ONE. Huh?

MAN TWO. What he do?

MAN ONE *(Looking at Fredric.)* The fuck you looking at? *(Pause.)* What the fuck you looking at huh? *(Pause.)*

FREDRIC. Nothing.

MAN ONE. Then look at nothing. *(Pause.)* Fucking faggot. *(Pause. Man One keeps looking at Fredric.)*

LILIAN. *(Whispering, looking at floor.)* Don't. *(Man One stares at Fredric.)*

MAN ONE. Kick your fucking face in. *(Fredric looks down at floor. Man One keeps looking at him. Woman enters with metallic pieces of junk hanging off her.)*

WOMAN WITH JUNK. *(In a loud monotone.)* Ladies and gentlemen hello, ladies and gentlemen good evening, ladies and gentlemen I am not here to beg, ladies and gentlemen I am from Venus Planet *yes.* Venus Planet is the planet of LOVE. The Man loves the Woman the Woman loves the Man. Ladies and gentlemen help send me home. Ladies and gentlemen, national anthem of Venus Planet. *(She bangs on junk randomly with stick. Silence. Man One keeps looking at Fredric. Train sound grows louder. Hold tableau.)*

SCENE SIX

Street. Speaker, Passerbys.

SPEAKER. "Babylon is fallen, is fallen; and all the graven images of her gods he hath broken unto the ground." Oh yes. Babylon is fallen my friends, that great city and all its works. In Babylon the buildings towered, yes my friends, in Babylon the people filled the shops, the taverns and the brothels, they wrapped themselves in cloths of vanity and lust. The stones of Babylon were thrown down. And why my friends. Ask *yourselves* why ... *(Fredric and Lilian enter.)*

FREDRIC. Oh man.

SPEAKER. "Have ye not known?"

LILIAN. Calm down.

SPEAKER. "Have ye not heard?"

FREDRIC. I should of ...

LILIAN. No.

SPEAKER. "Hath it not been *told* to you ..."

FREDRIC. Push his teeth ...

SPEAKER. "... from the *beginning?*"

LILIAN. That wouldn't have —

FREDRIC. Push his head under the, the —

SPEAKER. But the people of Babylon ...

LILIAN. Just forget about —

FREDRIC. — the *wheels* watch it pop ...

SPEAKER. ... did *not* listen, no.

FREDRIC. ... I'd laugh and kick it down the fucking sewer.

LILIAN. Stop it, that's horrible.

SPEAKER. Not until the *last.*

FREDRIC. Oh, it's okay some guy talks filth in your face —

LILIAN. Shut up, there's people around.

SPEAKER. Where are *your* thoughts, my friends?

FREDRIC. — then I have to protect you —

LILIAN. That's what you think?

SPEAKER. *Are* they with the Lord?

FREDRIC. That's the way things *are* and —

LILIAN. I ride the train every day —

SPEAKER. *Are* they wild in Babylon?

FREDRIC. — if you don't wanna *see* that —

SPEAKER. *Which* city do you live in?

LILIAN. But five minutes with you —

FREDRIC. Then I am *sorry* but you should not be here because —

LILIAN. I DIDN'T LOOK AT HIM.

SPEAKER. The city of the plain?

FREDRIC. What?

SPEAKER. Or the city on the hill?

LILIAN. You looked *right at him.* Everybody knows you don't look at anybody. You're so *smart* about the city, why don't you know that?

SPEAKER. *You have to choose!*

FREDRIC. Well I tell you what, take care of your own fucking self.

LILIAN. I *will.*

SPEAKER. "Not now," you say ...

FREDRIC. 'Cause I'm sick of it.

SPEAKER. "... I don't have *time* now ..."

LILIAN. Drag me down here —

FREDRIC. Living in a *fantasy* world —

SPEAKER. "... Can't you see I'm in a rush?"

LILIAN. And I hope you don't get *paid.*

SPEAKER. Oh *yes* I see ...

LILIAN. And I give you a *present,* you don't even say thank you, what is that?

FREDRIC. *(Exiting.)* Fuck this.

SPEAKER. ... but where are you rushing?

LILIAN. *Walk* away.

FREDRIC. I am.

SPEAKER. There are only two roads.

LILIAN. *(Calling after.)* Don't come back. Don't *see* me again.

SPEAKER. Which have you taken?

LILIAN. You have my money! *(To onlooking Passerbys.)* Yes,

it's a free show, everybody watch. *(She walks off. Fredric re-enters.)*

SPEAKER. "For here we have no continuing city ..."
FREDRIC. Lilian ... Come on, I'm ...
SPEAKER. "... but seek one ...
FREDRIC. don't ...
SPEAKER. "... to come."
FREDRIC. Lilian ...
PASSERBY. Ya ya ya, shut the fuck up. *(Another Passerby laughs. Fredric stands there.)*
SPEAKER. The city to come, my friends ... *(Fredric exits.)* *Not* this. *Not* here. *Not* now. The city that's to come. We read in Jeremiah —

SCENE SEVEN

A crowd of spectators on the street. Police barricade.

SPECTATOR ONE. Anything?
SPECTATOR TWO. Not yet.
MAN WITH CAMERA. Your picture for a dollar. Your picture for a dollar ...
SPECTATOR THREE. Could you move over? Sir?
SPECTATOR FOUR. No room.
SPECTATOR THREE. If you just took a step —
SPECTATOR FOUR. I have been here since four o'clock.
MAN WITH CAMERA. Picture for a dollar, who wants to be beautiful?
SPECTATOR ONE. Let's get one.
SPECTATOR TWO. You kidding? That's just a scam. *(To Man with Camera.)* Get outta here.
SPECTATOR FIVE. That man is hanging off the pole, officer. Officer ... *(Pause.)* I'm doing it too.
LILIAN. Excuse me ... excuse me please ...
MAN WITH CAMERA. I take your picture for a dollar ... you know you need it ...

LILIAN.   Going to the train ...

ROSE.   Quit shoving!

LILIAN.   Rose?

ROSE.   Oh. Oh. Hi ...

LILIAN.   What's going on?

ROSE.   I got here too *late.*

LILIAN.   Was there an accident?

SPECTATOR FIVE.   Somebody's on the ledge.

SPECTATOR THREE.   It was a car crashed.

MAN WITH CAMERA.   Yes, pretty lady, you need a picture now.

ROSE.   Come on, we have to get up front.

LILIAN.   I don't want to see that.

ROSE.   No, no, come *on. (She starts pushing.)*

SPECTATOR THREE.   Hey. Hey, fuck you.

ROSE.   Go to hell.

SPECTATOR THREE.   Some goddamn nerve, lady.

ROSE.   Just ignore him.

SPECTATOR THREE.   Sure, push right in.... Nobody cares, right, nobody's listening, I'm talking to myself.

LILIAN.   What are you doing, Rose?

ROSE.   They'll come down this way ... the theater's around the corner but there's a better view from here. I came by at lunch so I know.

LILIAN.   Who?

ROSE.   The *stars.* The *stars* are coming.

LILIAN.   What stars?

ROSE.   The *premiere.* The *movie.*

SPECTATOR FOUR.   Jeffrey Montane is a young man come to town to make good for himself. He's grown up on a farm, or some similar type of rural setting, and has never visited the city. After being lured to a show in which girls dressed as skyscrapers dance onstage in a provocative manner, he becomes lost in a crowded arcade where fast talking people try to sell him things. He enters a bar for directions, where a girl, a wisecracking brunette played of course by Rosalind Gillette, is being bullied by a man in a double-breasted suit.

LILIAN.   *(To Rose.)* You know this guy?

SPECTATOR FOUR.   Montane bravely steps in and a fight ensues in which he is knocked unconscious. The spunky Gillette becomes furious and decks the man with a round-house punch. When Montane comes to, she allows him to think he won, thanking him profusely. There follow several scenes in which they tour the town, encountering smart-aleck bus drivers, stuffy matrons, and comic ethnic types. Finally, at Ocean Park, they kiss on the boardwalk while the city glows in the distance. Then, suddenly, she runs away.

LILIAN.   She's married.

SPECTATOR FOUR.   No.

LILIAN.   She has a disease?

SPECTATOR FOUR.   No no.

ROSE.   She's really *rich* and he doesn't know it.

SPECTATOR FOUR.   Exactly.

ROSE.   But she's unhappy 'cause up in her penthouse she's cut off from life. And the guy in the suit, who's her fiancee only she doesn't love him, tells her she's throwing herself away on this clown from the sticks and what'll she do, live in a shack and grow corn, he doesn't think so, the city's in her blood. And Jeff Montane, when he finds out she's loaded, he gets really pissed, 'cause even though he's poor he's proud, he's going back to East Horselips or whatever. So —

SPECTATOR FOUR.   Her father, a prominent financier who only wants to make his daughter happy, has the police commissioner pretend to arrest Montane —

ROSE.   Until she can *talk* to him. But *Jeff* gets mistaken for an arch criminal who's like an identical twin so he has to escape with some other criminals who're scary but also funny.

SPECTATOR FOUR.   Following a bank rob —

ROSE.   Then a big chase with fire trucks and fruit wagons —

SPECTATOR FOUR.   A passing clergyman —

ROSE.   — but it all works out and in the end Jeff and Rosalind meet in Columbia Square, right in the middle of the street —

SPECTATOR FOUR.   The young couple, reunited —

ROSE.   They smooch like forever, everybody starts honking their horns and yelling, but they don't hear a thing, and

23

that's how it goes.

LILIAN.   You saw it already?

ROSE.   They wrote it up in the magazines.

SPECTATOR FOUR.   It's a fairly typical example of the genre.

LILIAN.   What?

SPECTATOR FOUR.   I am a student of film. I have a complete record of all motion pictures I have seen for the last ten years, along with their casts, production crews, and running times.

LILIAN.   Well, isn't that —

SPECTATOR FOUR.   It is important to me that a picture have a crowd scene. In such scenes I have come to realize that certain patterns repeat themselves, and that these patterns are directed at me.

LILIAN.   I'm sorry?

SPECTATOR FOUR.   Two people will for instance be conversing in the background in a restaurant scene, and it becomes obvious that they are talking about me. In some cases they will be visibly gesturing to where I am sitting. Or a man playing a messenger will deliver an envelope to a concert pianist, and the name on it will be mine. This has happened twice.

ROSE.   *(Under her breath.)* Ah Jesus he's nuts.

SPECTATOR FOUR.   I do not know why these films are addressing me. But they have made it clear that I am someone important. Although I may seem invisible I am important. They know I am here. They know I matter. These experiences have shown that to be true, and it is a great comfort. Do you understand this?

LILIAN.   Yes.

SPECTATOR FOUR.   Thank you. *(He turns away.)*

LILIAN.   *(To Rose.)* I'm going.

ROSE.   Just wait till they come.

LILIAN.   I don't want to be next to this guy.

ROSE.   Sure, so leave me here.

LILIAN.   I thought you had a *date.*

ROSE.   Huh? No, I never said that.

LILIAN. See you tomorrow.

ROSE. I have to tell you something.

LILIAN. What.

ROSE. Promise to stay.

LILIAN. What is it?

ROSE. You know.

LILIAN. No I don't.

ROSE. Something you did at work.

SPECTATOR ONE. There they are!

LILIAN. What do you mean?

ROSE. Hold on.

LILIAN. This is crazy ...

ROSE. Watch your elbow!

SPECTATOR TWO. I'm not *touching* you.

LILIAN. Who saw me at work?

ROSE. Huh? Stop pushing ...

SPECTATOR THREE. Move up, come on.

LILIAN. Oh, my heel ...

ROSE. I am not budging. I am *not budging*. I'm gonna see
this goddamn thing. I'm gonna be right out front for *once*
and I don't *care* who — HEY, JEFF! JEFF MONTANE! *(To
Lilian.)* He's short, isn't he, really short ... *(Out.)* LOOK
OVER HERE! LOOK AT ME! *(To Lilian.)* He's just a guy
from the city you know, he could be anybody ... *(Out.)* JEFF.
HEY JEFF. JEFF, LOOK AT *ME*, YOU BASTARD! OH
PLEASE PLEASE PLEASE LOOK AT ME! GODDAMN! *(To
Lilian.)* Help me yell.

LILIAN. No.

ROSE. Yes, you have to! JEFF! JEFF! OVER HERE!

LILIAN. OVER HERE, JEFF.

ROSE. LOOK AT US JEFF ... Oh this is fun ...

LILIAN and ROSE. LOOK AT US, LOOK AT US LOOK
AT US ...

ROSE. It's going to work, it's going to ... YES! YES! YES!
I LOVE YOU, JEFF, MY NAME IS ROSE. I LOOOVE
YOOUUU!

LILIAN. HELLO, JEFF, HELLO! *(Pause.)* HELLO. *(Pause.)*

ROSE. He saw us. He definitely saw us.

LILIAN. Look at my shoe now.

ROSE. There was a connection. Like a zing, I could feel it. He's gonna think about me. He's gonna look up and down the city for me and, no, that's too much like the movie, right, okay how about —

LILIAN. What did you hear at work?

ROSE. Uh, look, it's no big deal —

LILIAN. What.

ROSE. Somebody said they saw you take something.

LILIAN. No I didn't.

ROSE. That's what I said, the register tape got screwed up.

LILIAN. I didn't take anything, Rose.

ROSE. I know you didn't.

LILIAN. Who saw me?

ROSE. I don't know, Kraus came over and I said no, the lady bought the watch. *(Pause.)* So he wants to see you in the morning. *(Pause.)* Things disappear all the time from that store, they can't prove it. *(Pause.)*

LILIAN. I lost my job.

ROSE. Nah.

LILIAN. Yes. *God* I'm an idiot. What am I gonna do. *(Pause.)*

ROSE. You need a drink.

LILIAN. No.

ROSE. You need a few drinks. And tomorrow, *here's* what you do.

LILIAN. What.

ROSE. You go up there and lie through your teeth.

LILIAN. I can't.

ROSE. It's no big *deal.*

LILIAN. That makes it worse.

ROSE. It makes it *better.* That's why people *do* it. See this scarf? I walked out with it four months ago.

LILIAN. Really.

ROSE. Jesus, what they pay us, you better steal. Am I right?

LILIAN. You're right.

ROSE. I *am* right. That's how it goes in the city. Okay?

SPECTATOR THREE. Here comes Rosalind Gillette!

LILIAN. *(Not watching.)* Yes. *(Crowd cheers.)*

SCENE EIGHT

Back alley. Service door. Fredric, Waiter One.

WAITER ONE.   *(Smoking cigarette.)* Name a street.

FREDRIC.   Huh?

WAITER ONE.   Name any street in the city. *(Pause.)*

FREDRIC.   Washington.

WAITER ONE.   North or South.

FREDRIC.   North.

WAITER ONE.   North Washington Street. When I was fourteen years old I worked for a print jobber on North Washington Street. The paper I had to unload. Big rolls from the truck. Two, three hundreds pounds, I don't know. Onto handcarts six dollars a day. They were putting in the subway then. Down the middle of the street a huge crack, deep inside men working, when the dynamite went off you felt your stomach thump. I was always proud. My city. The things that were possible ...

FREDRIC.   Uh-huh ...

WAITER ONE.   Around the clock they worked. To build this thing. One day they hit a gas main. And something, they never knew, a cigarette, a spark ... a hammer against a rock .... Terrible, terrible. Some of them burned where they stood, others thrown seventy, eighty feet. Blown to pieces. I mean that, in pieces. You ride the train today, who bothers to consider ... *(Pause.)* Also a roller rink. I would go there with a girl. If I was lucky she couldn't skate, she'd have to hold on to me. *(Pause.)* You follow the principle?

FREDRIC.   What's the principle.

WAITER ONE.   History. What, all this just happened? No. There was a time, I remember for instance, a man would not leave his apartment without a hat I don't care a carton a milk. It was not done. And around you other men in hats, and you would think, all right, there's a *code*, this is how we agree to get along. Now of course ...

FREDRIC.   What stinks out here?

WAITER ONE.   They're not picking up the trash. *(Waiter Two enters.)*

WAITER TWO.   Hey, the flying dishman.

FREDRIC.   How's it going.

WAITER TWO.   It's dead. It's death. We got nothing. Nobody's spending nowhere.

WAITER ONE.   Thursday like a Monday.

WAITER TWO.   You working?

FREDRIC.   I got stuff lined up.

WAITER TWO.   Later for this dive, right?

FREDRIC.   Good riddance.

WAITER TWO.   You know it. How's that girl?

FREDRIC.   Who.

WAITER TWO.   Use to come for you.

FREDRIC.   She's around.

WAITER TWO.   Uh-huh.

FREDRIC.   On my *case.*

WAITER TWO.   Who needs it, huh.

FREDRIC.   I mean I love her —

WAITER TWO.   Woman in the city man, that's a whole nother *job.*

FREDRIC.   Better off on your own, huh.

WAITER TWO.   You go *home,* you gotta go to *work.* Put in some *time* or else.

WAITER ONE.   We all like attention.

FREDRIC.   I don't *have* time. Not right now. She can't understand —

WAITER TWO.   What it is, they're making the clocks shorter.

WAITER ONE.   Theory of Negativity.

FREDRIC.   Getting my life simple, you know, so I can start … moving *up.*

WAITER TWO.   Low to the ground and all around town.

FREDRIC.   Yeah, that's what … yeah.

WAITER TWO.   You'll do okay.

FREDRIC.   I think I will. *(Pause.)* So's he here?

WAITER TWO.   He's *here,* he's always here, does he wanna look at you?

FREDRIC.   I came to get my money.

WAITER TWO.   Yeah, well ...

FREDRIC.   What's the mood?

WAITER TWO.   Oh, he's happy, he's very happy.

WAITER ONE.   Listen, you learn to live with anything.

FREDRIC.   Jeez, I don't care.

WAITER TWO.   That's the spirit.

FREDRIC.   I mean he owes me, that's that, the bastard.

WAITER TWO.   He's a fat fuck.

WAITER ONE.   Shh.

WAITER TWO.   I'll tell it to his face, I don't care, right?

FREDRIC.   *And* he said I could waiter two nights a week.

WAITER TWO.   He did?

FREDRIC.   Why I took the job. He promised.

WAITER TWO.   Huh. *(Pause. To Waiter One.)* So I hit the exacta.

WAITER ONE.   That's good.

WAITER TWO.   We're talking a system. Okay, take any quarter stretch — *(Manager enters.)*

MANAGER.   Nobody needs to work, huh.

WAITER TWO.   Mr. Meese, we're dumping garbage —

MANAGER.   A customer asks me for more coffee.

WAITER TWO.   I —

MANAGER.   No, don't *say* anything. Do your job. *(Pause.)* Do your job or get out. *(Two exits. Manager looks at One.)* And you're supposed to be on a break.

WAITER ONE.   That is correct. *(Pause.)*

MANAGER.   Keep an eye on the time.

WAITER ONE.   Hunh. *(Manager starts in.)*

FREDRIC.   Mr. Meese, excuse me.

MANAGER.   Who's talking.

FREDRIC.   Um ...

MANAGER.   Who is this talking at me.

FREDRIC.   I came for my pay, sir.

MANAGER.   What is he.

FREDRIC.   The busboy.

MANAGER.   I don't know this.

FREDRIC.   I worked here. You owe me the last week.

(Pause.)

MANAGER.　The one who broke the dishes.

FREDRIC.　No I didn't.

MANAGER.　That comes out the salary, I told you that.

FREDRIC.　You're thinking somebody else, Mr. Meese. You said I could wait tables.

MANAGER.　And always coming in late.

FREDRIC.　I was late *twice.*

MANAGER.　I know you. You're a troublemaker. I don't need that kind of attitude. I remember you very well.

FREDRIC.　What's my name?

MANAGER.　That's right, the smart ass. I don't want the smartasses. A hundred smartasses I get coming in here every day. Every week a million smartasses jumping off the bus. This town don't need the smartasses. The smartass goes nowhere.

FREDRIC.　I want my pay.

MANAGER.　Is my advice to you.

FREDRIC.　You owe me for a week.

MANAGER.　I don't hear any of this.

FREDRIC.　I need the money, Mr. Meese, it's important.

MANAGER.　*(To Waiter One.)* Don't forget your tables.

FREDRIC.　*(Stepping towards Manager.)* Goddamn it, I *worked* for you —

MANAGER.　Hey hey. What is this. *(Pause.)*

FREDRIC.　Pay me.

MANAGER.　One more step, I'll have the cops like that. I never saw you sneaking back here? I didn't know what you were up to, you couldn't carry a tray? Call the cops, they find that crap in your pockets, you go to jail. That's all. *(Pause.)* I don't want to see you here again. *(He exits.)*

FREDRIC.　I'll burn this place *down.* I'll break the *windows.* Mr. *Meese.* Hey. *(Pause.)* Shit.

WAITER ONE.　If I was a young man today, I tell you honestly, I would avoid the restaurant field. It makes a person tense. *(Fredric looks at him. Pause.)* You come back in a few days. He won't remember. Come back, dress nicely, be polite

30

... you'd be surprised. I recall — *(Fredric exits. Waiter One looks at his watch, carefully stubs out cigarette, and goes inside.)*

SCENE NINE

A bar. Rose, Lilian.

ROSE. Sir! Sir! *(Young Waiter breezes by.)* Are you gonna have another?

LILIAN. I don't think so. I'm very warm.

ROSE. Have another, I'm having another. Sir!

LILIAN. I don't want to drink too much.

ROSE. I don't either, but I'm doing it. Am I complaining? Sir! Hey! *(Young Waiter goes by.)* What's with him?

LILIAN. He can't hear you.

ROSE. *(Looks at Lilian.)* Oh will you cheer *up?* It'll be all right.

LILIAN. I'm thinking about my *boyfriend.*

ROSE. That's very polite.

LILIAN. We broke up.

ROSE. When.

LILIAN. Tonight. I think.

ROSE. You *think?*

LILIAN. I don't know. I mean I don't care if see him again.

ROSE. Good. He's a creep.

LILIAN. Don't say that.

ROSE. He *is.* I remember him. He looks all chewed up.

LILIAN. Well sometimes he does.

ROSE. Like a dog was biting his head.

LILIAN. He gets cheap haircuts. He buys shoes off racks on the sidewalk. Plus he acts like he knows everything, and he *doesn't,* he doesn't know anything. And the really horrible thing is, oh god I can't say this, I thought when I met him, well, with someone around I'll be less afraid, you know, in the city, but I'm not. I'm more afraid. He's made me more

31

afraid. *(Pause.)* Why is the heat so high? *(She sips her drink.)*

ROSE. Look. Look. I know you a few months, right?

LILIAN. Yes.

ROSE. Let me tell you what your problem is.

LILIAN. What.

ROSE. You are from Outta Town.

LILIAN. Thanks so much.

ROSE. No, where're you from? You're from, uh ...

LILIAN. Middleboro.

ROSE. Middleboro, Middleboro, so this would be, what —

LILIAN. About twenty —

ROSE. Lawns, old ladies baking pies, everybody knows your name?

LILIAN. It's not *that* small.

ROSE. See, I can tell, there's not the *thing*.

LILIAN. What *thing*.

ROSE. The thing, the thing, the city thing.

LILIAN. Oh please.

ROSE. Nah, I watch you, it's like, "uh-oh, I hope nobody tells my *parents* —"

LILIAN. I hope nobody *does*.

ROSE. Well this is the difficulty. You need to take the Pledge of Allegiance.

LILIAN. What for.

ROSE. So you belong. Don't you want to belong?

LILIAN. I want them to get some *air* in here.

ROSE. Okay, raise your hand. Come on. It's good for you. *(Lilian raises hand.)* City Pledge of Allegiance. Repeat after me. "I do solemnly swear ..."

LILIAN. "I solemnly swear ..."

ROSE. "That, um, um ...

LILIAN. Come on, let's hear it ...

ROSE. "That nothing matters ..."

LILIAN. "That nothing matters ..."

ROSE. "... and *every*thing sucks," you have to say it.

LILIAN. "... and everything sucks."

ROSE. Feel better?

LILIAN. Oh yes, I'm happy now.

ROSE. Good. That means you have to have another drink.

LILIAN. All right. *(Pause. Young Waiter zips by.)*

ROSE. I can't *stand* places like this.

LILIAN. That's what I've been *saying*.

ROSE. He's ignoring us. Isn't he ignoring us?

LILIAN. He was snotty when we came *in*.

ROSE. Arrrgh. The attitude, you know? It makes me so, so ...

LILIAN. I know ...

ROSE. Like there's not enough already to put up with, every single day.

LILIAN. I waited half an hour for the bus this morning, then I couldn't get on?

ROSE. That's nothing. That doesn't even *count*. Were you ever on a bus that *exploded?*

LILIAN. No.

ROSE. I was.

LILIAN. What did you do?

ROSE. I *ran*. You ever see a man get shot?

LILIAN. No.

ROSE. I did. In the stomach. Right on the street in a fight. I saw a guy fall off a building when I was a kid. Someone once broke into my apartment, then every day for a year I got phone calls where they would just hang up. Does your roommate pray?

LILIAN. She might, I don't know.

ROSE. Mine does. Out *loud*. She asks me to *join in*. She leaves notes in the fridge, "Rose, Jesus loves you." What is that, a threat? I mean, just pay your goddamn half of the rent, you know?

LILIAN. Right.

ROSE. And stay out of my *life*. Plus they broke a pipe I haven't had hot water in a week.

LILIAN. I hate that, you never feel clean.

ROSE. And god oh god you know how you're sitting, do you ever feel this way, lying on your bed, your tiny bed in your little room, 'cause you can't sleep and around you, beneath you on top of you people, other people people people, you think what's he doing up there, always thumping two in the morning, and behind you, right in your ear, one inch of wall, someone's toilet, but like *right in the room*, I mean *you hear him sitting there*, out*side* some fuckhead yelling pissing in a doorway you have to get *up* in two hours I want to open the window and scream FUCK YOU, fuck *you*, who the FUCK DO YOU THINK YOU ARE.

LILIAN.   Well, it's —

ROSE.   YOU ARE NOT THE ONLY PERSON IN THIS CITY. No. You are NOT. Then at work, the train whatever everybody's stupid and crazy, everybody looks sick and pale some guy blows his nose onto the *floor* he looks at you like go fuck yourself, what do you think but he's got a *knife* a *gun* he'll rob me he'll rape me he'll kill me and NO ONE WILL CARE.

LILIAN.   All right Rose —

ROSE.   So okay, you, go to a party and you don't know anybody, they're all creepy and fashionable they treat you like death 'cause you don't know some stupid song and you look at yourself —

LILIAN.   Could you just stop —

ROSE.   And your clothes are *ugly*, your hair is *ugly*, you are an *ugly person* you shop in cheap stores you work as someone else's *slave* you take shit because you are *poor* and *afraid* and you have *nothing* going *nowhere* in *this horrible city* —

LILIAN.   *Stop it.*

ROSE.   Huh?

LILIAN.   You have to stop.

ROSE.   Why?

LILIAN.   It's not funny, you're upsetting me —

ROSE.   What?

LILIAN.   *It isn't funny.*

ROSE.   I'm not trying to make you *laugh*. I'm *talking*. Maybe someone *else* has a problem, y'ever think about that? Maybe you're not the only person who ... *(Pause.)*

LILIAN.   What? *(Pause.)* What is it? *(Pause.)* What are you crying for?

ROSE.   How the fuck would I know? *(Young Waiter enters with champagne in bucket.)*

LILIAN.   What's this?

YOUNG WAITER.   Champagne.

LILIAN.   What? We didn't order this.

YOUNG WAITER.   Compliments of, uh ... that guy. *(He points to Diamond a few feet away, who nods.)*

LILIAN.   Who? *(Young Waiter pops cork.)* No, don't do that, we don't want it.

YOUNG WAITER.   Look, it's already *opened.*

LILIAN.   I don't care, send it back. And tell that man ... Excuse me, are you listening?

YOUNG WAITER.   *What.*

LILIAN.   Tell that man that, uh, uh ...

ROSE.   I'd like some.

LILIAN.   Rose, no.

ROSE.   I would like some champagne. *(To Young Waiter.)* Go ahead, please. Tell him thank you very much. *(Young Waiter exits.)* I'm doing what I want from now on.

LILIAN.   Well that's considerate.

ROSE.   Oh don't pretend to be *hurt.* You don't care about anyone anyway.

LILIAN.   Then I'll leave.

ROSE.   You would, wouldn't you. You'd just leave your only friend here with a strange man.

LILIAN.   Oh, Jesus, what do you want from me, Rose?

ROSE.   I don't want to be alone. *Please. (Diamond comes over.)*

DIAMOND.   Ladies, let me say this. May I? I mean, what, do you mind? Just say so. Yes, no?

LILIAN.   What?

DIAMOND.   I don't know you, this is obvious, you don't know me, which would follow, I could tell you a lot about myself, look, who couldn't, last thing we need now is another *story,* am I right? Okay. So. I see two ladies, two lovely which I mean nothing by it young ladies, all I want to do, certainly no offense, a gesture to say god bless you, you're lovely, and, uh, are you enjoying it?

ROSE.   Oh, the —

DIAMOND.   Just a little expression —

ROSE.   Yes, thank you.

DIAMOND.   So you're enjoying the drink, this gives me pleasure. Now tell me and I don't mean to pry, I see you sitting here, young ladies as you are, it wouldn't surprise me you're waiting for someone, young men, young people like yourselves, would it be that terrible, I genuinely want to know, would you mind that much if I joined you?

ROSE.   Why not?

DIAMOND.   Miss? *(Lilian doesn't answer.)* Look, I can imagine what you're thinking, let me tell you one thing about myself, I'm short, I'm bald, I'm fat.

LILIAN.   What kind of thing is that to say?

DIAMOND.   Do I know, I'm only talking, how do I know what I mean? *(Lilian looks at him, then laughs.)* Ah, that's lovely, you have a lovely laugh, can I sit?

LILIAN.   Oh, sure. What's the difference.

DIAMOND.   *(Sitting.)* Oh sure, she says, corner of the mouth, I like that, a real city girl.

LILIAN.   You think so, huh?

DIAMOND.   I could see right off.

ROSE.   What about me?

DIAMOND.   You. Give me a second. You ever been to Egypt?

ROSE.   How come?

DIAMOND.   I'm thinking a certain Cleopatra ... *(Rose makes a face.)* What, I'm allowed my opinions. Aaron! Over here! This is a friend of mine, you'll like him a lot, Aaron, please, over here, I want you to meet two very charming young people, what's your name, did you already tell me?

ROSE.   Rose.

DIAMOND.   Rose and ...

LILIAN.   Lilian.

DIAMOND.   Rose and Lilian. Two lovely flowers.

ERENHART.   How do you do.

DIAMOND.   So sit down, join the discussion, what were we talking about?

LILIAN.   We weren't talking about anything.

DIAMOND.   Oh, she's tough, I'm telling you, like asphalt. So let's talk about something. Let's talk about, uh ...

ERENHART. I'm afraid I'll have to leave in a few —

DIAMOND. Nah, come on, the tab's on me.

ERENHART. I can't let you do that.

DIAMOND. Aaron, allow me the privilege.

ERENHART. You've done plenty, Dave, believe me —

DIAMOND. No no, this isn't business —

ERENHART. *(To Lilian.)* I'm very sorry ...

DIAMOND. Business is over and we are *enjoying* ourselves, am I right, ladies?

ROSE. What business are you in?

DIAMOND. I'll tell you honestly, sometimes I'd say the monkey business. Ha? You know? Lilian, that's an empty glass.

LILIAN. I don't care for any, thank you.

DIAMOND. Rose, are you ready?

ROSE. Well, just a little.

ERENHART. I'm afraid we, uh ...

LILIAN. Excuse me?

ERENHART. Nothing, I just, I'm afraid we're looking to celebrate.

LILIAN. Celebrate what?

ERENHART. We, uh ...

DIAMOND. Whatever you want, what do you want to celebrate?

ROSE. Sympathetic friends.

LILIAN. Ha ha.

DIAMOND. I say we celebrate being in the greatest town on earth, how about that?

ROSE. All right.

DIAMOND. I mean it's a *hell* of a thing. I say god bless, I look out the window some night I think every light's a person, huh? Some son of a gun looking to unload what he got, somebody else looking to get it, which is perfect, it clicks, it hums, it works, it's a *melody*. You know what I mean?

ROSE. You're saying every light you see ...

LILIAN. Is a person Rose, we all heard him.

ERENHART. I didn't know you were poetic, Dave.

DIAMOND. You hear what he called me? This guy's got some nerve, I oughta, no, I'm joking, of course, Aaron, please, drink, come on, you're making me nervous. Go ahead. *(Pause. Erenhart sips from glass.)*

ERENHART. I'm drinking.

DIAMOND. All right then. *(Silence.)*

ROSE. I know a poem.

DIAMOND. Of course, let's hear it.

ROSE. Um, okay, okay ...
"The Owl and the Pussycat went to sea ..."

DIAMOND. Lovely.

ROSE. *"In a beautiful pea green boat;*
They took some honey, and plenty of money ..."

DIAMOND. Sure, you'd have to ...

ROSE. Shush ... Um, ah ...
"Wrapped up in a five pound note.
The Owl looked up to the stars above,
And sang to a small guitar,
O lovely Pussy, O Pussy my love,
What a beautiful Pussy you are!"

(Pause.)

DIAMOND. Huh. How about that. That's a hell of a thing. What's the last part?

ROSE. *"O lovely Pussy, O Pussy my love,*
What a beautiful Pussy ..."

(Pause. Laughing.) Oh, you, you're *naughty.*

DIAMOND. What I say?

ROSE. You're terrible. You really are.

DIAMOND. I'm an innocent man, save me!

ROSE. I don't think I will.

ERENHART. *"The City is of Night, but not of Sleep;*
There sweet sleep is not for the weary brain ..."

LILIAN. Excuse me?

ERENHART. All I ever know is two lines of something.

LILIAN. Sounds very ...

DIAMOND. Have another drink, professor.

LILIAN. You're a teacher?

ERENHART. No, he's just ... I work. For the city.

LILIAN. Huh.

ERENHART. It's not very interesting. *(Pause.)*

DIAMOND. What do you girls do?

ROSE. Guess.

DIAMOND. Well ... the way you said that poem, that took talent. *Oh* boy. Don't say you're actresses. Don't let me hear that.

ROSE. What if we were?

DIAMOND. Ladies. You don't know. The theater. This is my heart. This is my passion. I don't miss an opening night. Twenty years whatever the show and believe me I seen some stinkers, I saw that thing where they all run around a giant clock, I'll be frank, it left me very confused, well it's modern, right, so what do you want. Now the *old* days, the balcony, two dollars, great names, John Harperson, Blanche Palmer, oh what a crush I had, Larimer Duke, the man's voice a *shiver* went up my spine, oh the theaters, the Adelphi, the Forum Royale, Morgan's Pantheon, you remember this Aaron?

ERENHART. Little before my time.

DIAMOND. The heyday, the absolute heyday. Geez. Am I that old? *(Pause.)*

ROSE. Did you see *Happy Go Lucky?*

DIAMOND. Lovely show. Very entertaining. Beautiful music. *(Singing.)* La-da-daaa ...

ROSE. We were *almost* in that.

DIAMOND. You're kidding.

ROSE. That close.

DIAMOND. Tough game. You keep at it. I'll say I knew you when.

ROSE. I'll drink to that.

DIAMOND. *(Of empty bottle.)* That went quick. Who's for another? Lilian?

LILIAN. I'm afraid I can't afford it, I'm just a poor actress.

DIAMOND. No, no, it's all on me.

LILIAN. I couldn't let you do that.

DIAMOND. She couldn't let me!

ROSE. It's really nice of —

DIAMOND. Please, please, let me spend my money. You could make me smile, it's such a simple thing, I can tell you're a kind person, do a good deed.

ERENHART. Dave, she doesn't want to.

DIAMOND. Aaron, no, now, I'm talking with Lilian. Lilian, Lilian, Lilian.

LILIAN. What.

DIAMOND. I don't know. You look so sad. I think my heart's gonna break. *(Pause.)*

LILIAN. I'm not sad.

DIAMOND. Forgive me.

LILIAN. I'm happy. Ask Rose how happy I am. *(Pause.)*

ERENHART. We should go.

LILIAN. No. Um … let's have another bottle.

ROSE. Yeah, let's do that.

DIAMOND. That's what I'm *saying*. We don't do this now, what are we gonna laugh about in the morning, am I right?

LILIAN. I guess so.

DIAMOND. No no, none a that. Take a stand.

LILIAN. You are *right*.

DIAMOND. Okay. Now we're getting along. *(To Young Waiter.)* Hey you.

YOUNG WAITER. Yes sir.

DIAMOND. What is your name.

YOUNG WAITER. My name is Harold.

DIAMOND. Harold, these are your instructions. Bring us a new bottle here. When that bottle's done, bring us another and keep doing that till we fall down. Got it?

YOUNG WAITER. I think so, sir.

DIAMOND. *(Handing him a bill.)* Just in case, here's so you remember.

YOUNG WAITER. I'm on it right away, sir. *(He exits briskly.)*

DIAMOND. Look at that. That's a happy guy. He's happy, we're happy, everybody's happy. See how much fun everything can be? *(He laughs. Rose joins in. Lilian looks at Erenhart, and starts laughing too.)*

SCENE TEN

A hotel lobby. Fredric, Bill in booth behind wire screen, Man with Pants. Electric bell ringing in distance.

MAN WITH PANTS.   I went down, an I had the paper like you suppost ...
BILL.   Right ...
MAN WITH PANTS.   You show it, they give you a slip take it to the *agency* ...
BILL.   For assistance, I know.
MAN WITH PANTS.   Sistance agency, yeah, only they don't got the file, I waited *all* day, know what they say?
FREDRIC.   I don't work here, okay?
MAN WITH PANTS.   Say I got to show proof. I got to prove who I am. I mean sir. Young Sir. Just please. Can I ask you something?
FREDRIC.   What?
MAN WITH PANTS.   Who the hell else gonna wanna be me? *(Pause.)* This the *paper.*
BILL.   I understand. The room —
MAN WITH PANTS.   No *no.*
BILL.   The room is seven dollars. You see?
MAN WITH PANTS.   I *know* it, but —
BILL.   I'm not the boss, I can't.
MAN WITH PANTS.   I know you ain't the *boss.* I know your situation. I just want a *favor.*
BILL.   What.
MAN WITH PANTS.   Look what I got here. *(He reaches into shirt and pulls out bundle. He carefully unrolls it, revealing a pair of pants.)* They brand new.
BILL.   I'm sorry. I don't need —
MAN WITH PANTS.   It cold outside.
FREDRIC.   We're already wearing pants.
MAN WITH PANTS.   That's what I'm *saying.* I got to *change.* *(Pause. To Bill.)* I got to change my pants. I got the new nice pants and I just got to change 'em. Cop see me on the street

41

king off my pants you know how it goes. Let me change **my pants**, man. Just someplace warm to change my pants. Let **me** do that. *(Pause.)*

FREDRIC.   What's the *bell?*

BILL.   Elevator.

FREDRIC.   Is it stuck?

BILL.   No. Probably the kids. City's paying for a couple of families, kids like to ring the bell. Can't be more than six or seven, they should be asleep. At this hour ... *(Pause. He looks at Man With Pants.)* Go up in the corner there.

MAN WITH PANTS.   God bless you man.

BILL.   That's all right.

MAN WITH PANTS.   God seeing everything and he gonna bless you.

BILL.   Just go ahead. *(Man goes up into corner and starts changing pants.)*

FREDRIC.   Jesus, the smell.

BILL.   I know.

FREDRIC.   How can a person smell like that?

BILL.   It's not his fault.

FREDRIC.   He could wash somewhere. A fire hydrant or whatever. A piece of soap, take it from a men's room, they never notice. That's what I'd do.

BILL.   I suppose.

FREDRIC.   You have a choice. You decide how you want it to be. My pop?

BILL.   Hmm.

FREDRIC.   I don't think he bought a bar of soap in his life, he snuck it outta restaurants. Embarrassed the piss outta me. Pockets full of little soap bars, matchbooks, shoe horns, whatever looked free. "Just in case," huh?

BILL.   Right.

FREDRIC.   Smart though. He knew the city. Worked three jobs at once and I never heard him moan. Guys like this ... *(He looks at Man With Pants.)* I'm sorry, they don't try hard enough. You're not supposed to say that but ...

BILL.   Yes. *(Pause.)* Somebody died upstairs the other night.

42

FREDRIC.   People die?

BILL.   He was sick ... I don't know with what, very thin. They took him away, I changed the sheets, that's part of my job. I washed after that. My wife made me. It's silly, you can't get sick from a sheet, can you.

FREDRIC.   No. I don't ... no.

BILL.   That's what they say. *(Bell stops ringing. They watch Man With Pants change pants. Pause.)*

FREDRIC.   You like this better than the restaurant, Bill?

BILL.   I couldn't go on there.

FREDRIC.   What a sonofabitch, huh? You can't *work* for him.

BILL.   Here I'm the night man. Sometimes trouble but usually I'm left alone. When I get home my wife is waiting. I'm doing what I can. I'm trying to have some hope. *(Pause.)*

FREDRIC.   Maybe you could do me a favor.

BILL.   What is it?

FREDRIC.   I'm a little in the hole.

BILL.   Uh-huh.

FREDRIC.   You know I quit at the place —

BILL.   No, I didn't.

FREDRIC.   Yeah, I did that, I had an offer come up, much better deal, only turns out they're not opening for another, *month* or so?

BILL.   Right.

FREDRIC.   But I have to pay my *rent* ... and ...

BILL.   How much do you need?

FREDRIC.   How much can you spare?

BILL.   Well, I usually give all my money to my wife. She takes care of everything.

FREDRIC.   Uh-huh.

BILL.   She's very good with it, and I don't have to worry.

FREDRIC.   So you can't, uh ...

BILL.   I have subway fare, I have three dollars for a sandwich. I don't need that.

FREDRIC.   That's okay. I mean ... sure. Thanks. *(Pause.)* I'll take it. *(Bill hands him the money.)* They looking for anybody here?

BILL. I don't think so. I'll ask.

FREDRIC. 'Cause until I get started, some kind of temporary situation, a little extra cash ...

BILL. Sure.

FREDRIC. I mean anything. *(Pause.)*

BILL. Are you all right, Fred?

FREDRIC. Yeah. Course.

BILL. You're not in any trouble.

FREDRIC. No. I'm just, between things.

BILL. You don't mind my —

FREDRIC. No.

BILL. Because I think about other people, that I know, and losing touch —

FREDRIC. Yeah, I'm sorry, I've been —

BILL. No, but, that phrase, "losing *touch*," you ever think about it.

FREDRIC. Like how.

BILL. You lose touch, you don't feel anything. That's what it means. You don't feel anything about other people.

FREDRIC. Right.

BILL. That's a strange place to be. *(Pause. Bell starts ringing again.)*

FREDRIC. That's why I wanted to stop *in* ... say hello, and ... *(Pause.)* Elevator.

BILL. Yes. *(Pause.)*

FREDRIC. I better get going. I'll let you know if —

BILL. Did I ever show you a picture of my wife?

FREDRIC. No ...

BILL. *(Taking out photo.)* This is her. *(Fredric looks at it. Pause.)*

FREDRIC. She's ... pretty.

BILL. Do you think so?

FREDRIC. Yeah.

BILL. I don't know. I can't tell. *(Pause.)* I'm twice her age.

FREDRIC. Really.

BILL. She's not from here. She's from another country. She doesn't speak English very well.

FREDRIC. She'll pick it up.

BILL. Yes. She'll learn things. The city won't seem so strange to her. She won't need me so much ... *(Pause.)*

FREDRIC. I gotta go, Bill. Losing time. My girlfriend, uh ...

BILL. Right.

FREDRIC. Promised I'd meet her, you know she's ... you'd like her, she's a great.... I'll bring her around one day. We can all ...

BILL. I'd like that.

FREDRIC. Okay. *(Pause. Bell rings.)*

BILL. Fred. Um. I'm not supposed to leave the lobby. *(Pause.)*

FREDRIC. You want me to —

BILL. Just for a minute, I'm sorry, maybe they're stuck. *(Fredric looks at Man With Pants asleep in corner with pants half off.)* Let him sit there, I'll take care of it.

FREDRIC. Doesn't bother me. *(Bell rings.)*

BILL. One minute ... I'm sorry ... *(He exits. Bell continues ringing. Fredric stands in lobby, looking at Man With Pants.)*

FREDRIC. Hey. *(Man opens his eyes.)* Your pants.

MAN WITH PANTS. Huh.

FREDRIC. You wanted to change your pants. *(Man With Pants looks down at legs blankly. Pause.)*

MAN WITH PANTS. Yes, God bless you, young sir. *(Man With Pants pulls off other pants leg. His foot is swollen and discolored. He sees Fredric looking at it.)* That what Lincoln Head done. You know Lincoln Head? *(Fredric shakes his head.)* Lincoln Head. Abraham *Lincoln*. The *park*.

FREDRIC. Lincoln hurt your foot.

MAN WITH PANTS. Mess me all up. When I'm sleeping. His *head* come off. It *big*. It bigger than a normal head. Lincoln Head, man, it *this* big. Big Lincoln eye. Big Lincoln ear. Big scary Lincoln nose. Right on top of me I couldn't *breathe*. How much you think Lincoln Head weigh?

FREDRIC. I don't know.

MAN WITH PANTS. Hundred pound. Hundred *fifty* pound. Big old bronze Lincoln head break off the park middle of the night, mess up my ribs, my teeth, damn near kill me, police *grab* me say what you climbing all over Lincoln knocking off his head, that against the law. And judge go what you got in your defense, I tell him, sir, I never done nothing to Lincoln, that bastard jumped *me*. Huh?

FREDRIC.   Okay.

MAN WITH PANTS.   You like that.

FREDRIC.   Funny.

MAN WITH PANTS.   Funny yeah, watch out for that Lincoln.

FREDRIC.   You bet.

MAN WITH PANTS.   Come along mess up your life, he don't care. *(Pause.)* Young sir. You spare a little something. Be my friend, all right. You a good man. It cold tonight. Give a little hand, what you say, help me out ... *(Pause.)* Oh, look at me. Just look at me. That don't cost. *(Pause.)*

FREDRIC.   Next time.

MAN WITH PANTS.   That a promise?

FREDRIC.   Yeah. *(Pause.)*

MAN WITH PANTS.   Okay. I'm waiting for you. *(Man With Pants starts pulling on pants. Bell rings. Fredric takes out the five. Pause. He crumples it in his hand and exits.)*

SCENE ELEVEN

Observation deck of a skyscraper. Lilian and Rose with eyes closed, Diamond, Erenhart, Guard.

DIAMOND.   Ready? *(Rose and Lilian nod.)* Open your eyes. *(They do so. They take in the unseen panorama.)*

ROSE.   Wow.

DIAMOND.   It's something huh?

LILIAN.   Look at all the *lights* ...

DIAMOND.   You don't know the city till you seen it from up here.

ROSE.   My knees are weak.

LILIAN.   How high are we?

DIAMOND.   *(To Guard.)* Hey, ah, you ...

GUARD.   The observation deck is one thousand one hun-

46

dred and fifty six feet above the sea level.

ROSE. What's that mean?

GUARD. Huh?

ROSE. We're on top of the ocean or something?

GUARD. Um ... I think ...

ERENHART. Sea level is a standard used to measure height or depth. The level of the surface of the sea.

ROSE. Oh.

ERENHART. The city, the ground the city is on, has an average height of nine feet above sea level.

ROSE. Really.

ERENHART. Yes. Although in some places, for instance around Soldier's Plaza, it's actually sinking at a rate of half an inch a year. *(To Lilian.)* The bedrock, you see, gives way to sedimentary layers. Load factors were miscalculated and the area was over-built. So two centuries from now it could be underwater. *(Pause.)*

DIAMOND. You know what he's talking about?

ROSE. No.

DIAMOND. Good, I thought it was me.

LILIAN. The city is sinking?

ERENHART. Not exactly —

ROSE. Well I don't care. I think it's beautiful! Hello down there! *(She steps up on railing.)* Whoo, I'm drunk.

GUARD. Lady, you can't —

DIAMOND. Sure she can.

GUARD. See, I'm responsible, anybody here after closing —

DIAMOND. Who's gonna know, pally. Did you even see us?

GUARD. If I'm caught —

DIAMOND. I understand, this is concern you're showing. Believe me, you don't get a lot a that in this town. Now here's our nieces from the godforsaken heartland, never seen nothing taller than a moose, could we send them home they never went up the Sullivan Building, of course not, now look, I forgot to include this one. Here. *(He offers money.)* Add it to the pile. Come on. *(Pause. Guard takes money.)*

GUARD. I have to ask you be careful. Things could happen.

DIAMOND. Hey, don't I know, really, thanks a lot.

GUARD.   People come up here to kill themselves, eight, ten times a year.

DIAMOND.   What a shame.

GUARD.   They have the bars, but people want to kill themselves, you can't stop them.

DIAMOND.   How about that, huh? *(Rose starts giggling.)*

GUARD.   Once a lady tried to kill herself, the wind kept blowing her back on her behind, excuse me.

ROSE.   So she couldn't kill herself?

GUARD.   No, she couldn't kill herself once.

DIAMOND.   Yeah, look, we really just came for the view. *(Pause.)*

GUARD.   I'm right inside. I can hear everything.

DIAMOND.   Okay.

GUARD.   So when you are done —

DIAMOND.   No problem, thank you so much. *(Pause.)* *Thank* you. *(Guard goes inside.)* Geez, I hate a worrier. Where does it get you?

ROSE.   *Nowhere.*

DIAMOND.   Damn straight.

ROSE.   To hell with worriers. And waiters and customers and everybody else. Lilian, Lilian, look!

LILIAN.   What?

ROSE.   Down there. Down *there.* The sign, it's Tuckman's, you can see Tuckman's.

LILIAN.   I don't need to see that.

ROSE.   You're right. To hell with it! We're up here and you aren't so ... FUCK YOU!

DIAMOND.   Hoo boy, here we go!

ROSE.   Well why not.

DIAMOND.   Rose, you're a peach. Can a rose be a peach?

ROSE.   I can be anything!

DIAMOND.   Sure you can. Let's look at the river.

ROSE.   Oooh, we have to see the river, right *now!*

DIAMOND.   It's around the other side. *(Rose stumbles. Diamond catches her.)* Easy there.

ROSE.   I almost *fell.*

DIAMOND.   I know.

ROSE.   I almost fell off the *building.* Ooo, You think I could of *killed myself?*

DIAMOND.   *(Approvingly.)* You're a very sick girl. *(He starts leading her off.)*

ROSE.   Lilian, come look at the river.

LILIAN.   It's too windy. I'll stay here.

ROSE.   I hate you! No, I didn't mean that! Please?

DIAMOND.   She don't know what she's missing.

ROSE.   Oh the hell with her. *(To Lilian.)* You'll be sorry! *(They exit. Silence.)*

ERENHART.   Is this the first — ?

LILIAN.   Excuse me?

ERENHART.   Up here.

LILIAN.   No, my ... a friend took me.

ERENHART.   Ah.

LILIAN.   I didn't see anything. It was cloudy. There were school kids running around, we had a fight ...

ERENHART.   You fought with the kids?

LILIAN.   No. With my friend. *(Pause.)*

ERENHART.   Is acting difficult? *(Lilian laughs.)* You don't want to talk about it.

LILIAN.   I'm not an actress. *(Pause.)*

ERENHART.   I thought —

LILIAN.   She was just pretending. She likes fooling people ... it makes her feel better. Later on she'll laugh at them. I don't think that's right.

ERENHART.   Well she fooled me. Or you did.

LILIAN.   I didn't say anything.

ERENHART.   Maybe that's why. *(Pause.)*

LILIAN.   You ever go to Tuckman's?

ERENHART.   The store, no, not usually.

LILIAN.   That's where we work.

ERENHART.   What do you do there?

LILIAN.   A floater ... I float. Like if there's a line at a register, I open up another one. Or a sale in a department they need an extra person ... god this is boring.

ERENHART.   Not at all.

LILIAN.   It is. It's the most boring thing a person can do.

There's nothing else to say about it. *(Pause.)*

ERENHART. It must be good experience.

LILIAN. For what?

ERENHART. For ... the future. Moving up in the company.

LILIAN. Huh. I'm not going to be in Tuckman's all my life.

ERENHART. What is it you want to do?

LILIAN. I don't know. Something ... not boring. I could ... I don't know. I wish I was smart. Then I could do clever things, and I wouldn't have to work. But I'm not smart.

ERENHART. I'm sure you are.

LILIAN. No. I'm just ... *(Pause.)* I had a job showing apartments for a little while. Everybody said you could make a lot of money that way. But I wasn't any good at it. You don't get paid unless you make someone take the apartment. I couldn't. I didn't know what to say. They'd go, "It's very dark ... it's too small ... there's a funny smell in the drains ..." All these apartments, up back stairs, looking into alleys, on top of donut shops, you could just feel ... all the people who'd been in them, even with new paint, you could feel how they seeped into the walls.

ERENHART. Do you believe in ghosts?

LILIAN. Huh? No. There aren't any ghosts. There's just other people. *(Pause.)* I want to live someplace brand new. And really modern. Modern things, they're ... happy, you know? 'Cause they don't look like anybody made them. I want a modern place, really high up, like this. From down there I'd just be this little light, and nobody would know who I was, or what I'd be doing. They wouldn't know anything about me.

ERENHART. Would you be alone?

LILIAN. If I wanted to be.

ERENHART. What if you didn't?

LILIAN. There'd be someone there. I guess. *(Pause. Erenhart points out.)*

ERENHART. The big street down there? Away to the south?

LILIAN. Uh-huh.

ERENHART. That's the Concourse.

LILIAN. I know that.

ERENHART. It used to be called Terminal Street. All the trains had to stop there to be loaded onto barges before they could cross the river. That was before they built the tunnels. Earlier it was known as Tanner's Lane, because there'd once been a village on the spot, well outside the boundaries of the city, and what they did there was tan animal hides. It was on the shore of a pond, which the tanneries polluted. So the city drained it and turned it into a potter's field, where the poor were buried. Now there isn't room, they get cremated and the ash is dumped at sea. But when they dig a new foundation on the Concourse, they always turn up bones. And under the sub-basements the spring that fed the pond runs in a channel that hooks up with the sewer main. The Indians fished that pond. They caught them in their hands. That must be hard.

LILIAN. When did they do that?

ERENHART. Two hundred fifty, three hundred years ago.

LILIAN. Huh. All that happened? *(Erenhart nods.)* How come you know so much?

ERENHART. A hobby. I've always been interested. The city. How it grew. Changed.

LILIAN. I can't see it ever being different from now.

ERENHART. No, that's what's so, um, *fascinating.* To me. Because, well, look at this view, it's famous, isn't it. From every postcard. It just seems ... inevitable. Like a continent. But everything you can see from this spot, every brick, it's act of will. What is all this but a billion decisions piled one on top of another. Nothing happens here without a human thought. Nothing would exist if we didn't want it to. So ... this is what we want. *(Pause.)* I'm sorry, I'm not making any sense.

LILIAN. No, I'm just.... I need to go back down, it's very cold.

ERENHART. Take my jacket.

LILIAN. Then you'll freeze.

ERENHART. That's all right. *(He offers jacket. Lilian shakes her head.)* Please, I insist. *(Lilian takes it and drapes it over her shoulders.)*

51

LILIAN. Thank you. *(Rose shrieks from off-stage, then breaks into a peal of laughter. Pause.)* Didn't kill herself yet.

ERENHART. No. *(Pause.)*

LILIAN. Where in the city do you live, someplace nice, right.

ERENHART. I don't. Not anymore. I take the train in. Half hour ride. If I'm lucky.

LILIAN. That must be convenient.

ERENHART. Yes. It's convenient. *(Pause.)*

LILIAN. What are you and Mr. Diamond celebrating?

ERENHART. Mr. Diamond ... runs a manufacturing firm. They make reinforcement rods for concrete construction. The city is going build a sewage treatment plant. The agency I supervise is responsible for finding suppliers. Mr. Diamond's bid, his company's bid was accepted. Mr. Diamond is very happy about that, and ... this is his way of thanking me.

LILIAN. By giving you pneumonia a thousand feet above sea level.

ERENHART. That's not exactly how he sees it. *(Pause.)*

LILIAN. Building a what?

ERENHART. Sewage treatment. It's a big problem. The city's waste basically flows straight into the river. Should have been dealt with years ago, but nobody could agree on a plan. Twenty million spent and nothing built. Now it'll cost six times as much.

LILIAN. Where's the thought in that?

ERENHART. Ah yes. Well. Yes.

LILIAN. But you're going to fix it?

ERENHART. No, that's someone else's job. So fortunately they won't blame me.

LILIAN. For what?

ERENHART. The things that happen.

LILIAN. What things?

ERENHART. The things that will always happen. *(Pause.)* Ever think of working for the city?

LILIAN. No.

ERENHART. It's not hard. You just take the civil service exam.

LILIAN.   I'm not very good at exams.

ERENHART.   Can you read and write? Do you know the order of the alphabet?

LILIAN.   Most of it.

ERENHART.   You're ahead of the game. And it helps if you know somebody.

LILIAN.   I don't.

ERENHART.   You know me. *(Pause.)*

LILIAN.   Well ...

ERENHART.   No, I don't mean to be.... I'm just saying it's something to look into. If you're looking for a change. It can lead to things, there's a scale of promotion ...

LILIAN.   Thanks for the tip.

ERENHART.   I'm serious. I offer to help because ... I know how hard it is. And I can tell that you're somebody who's still looking for her place.

LILIAN.   What do you mean?

ERENHART.   Where you fit in. I know what that's like. To be here and feel that. You're not from the city, are you?

LILIAN.   No, but I've been —

ERENHART.   I could tell. Please forgive me. We're strangers and I don't mean to be rude. But I see you so clearly and that's ... that's rare. Can I ask how old you are? You don't have to say.

LILIAN.   Twenty-six.

ERENHART.   Young.

LILIAN.   No.

ERENHART.   You are.

LILIAN.   I don't feel it. I feel ... used up.

ERENHART.   By what.

LILIAN.   This. All of this. *(Pause.)* At work today, I stole something to give to ... I don't know why, I just did it. All I worried about was getting caught.

ERENHART.   What did you take?

LILIAN.   A watch. It's ridiculous. A cheap watch.

ERENHART.   Can you bring it back?

LILIAN.   No, I don't have it. I gave it to ... this guy. A guy I know. But he won't give it back. Not now. *(Pause.)* Manager wants to see me in morning ... *(Pause.)*

ERENHART. You meant to pay for it later.

LILIAN. No.

ERENHART. You put it aside and, just forgot. Anyone could understand how —

LILIAN. I'm going to tell the truth.

ERENHART. What's that.

LILIAN. I stole it. It was easy.

ERENHART. Will that help the situation?

LILIAN. If you can steal ... you can do anything. That's.... I don't want to think that. I ... *(Pause.)* Now I'm not making sense. *(Pause.)*

ERENHART. We rest our lives on the belief ... the *hope,* that our actions have effect on others ...

LILIAN. Right.

ERENHART. That we influence them, as they influence us. That these connections give us meaning. These other lives make us real.

LILIAN. I don't know. I don't know ...

ERENHART. But what do we learn, perhaps, what do we repeat to ourselves, in the end what becomes our consolation, "It doesn't matter ... it doesn't matter ... it doesn't matter what we do ..."

LILIAN. Like a hundred times a day.

ERENHART. And all the while we're changing, we don't even notice but we're changing into someone else. Someone who does things we never would. Who can be immersed in everyday scenes of violence and degradation and feel ... nothing. A flash of ... fear. Guilt. Relief. Nothing. *(Pause.)*

LILIAN. That's happening to me.

ERENHART. Yes.

LILIAN. I don't want it to. But it is. I know it is.

ERENHART. *(Looking out.)* I'll tell you from my heart, Lilian. This is the saddest place on earth. *(Pause. They look at each other. Lilian shivers.)* Still cold ...

LILIAN. It goes right through me. *(Erenhart steps up to her and puts his arms around her. Lilian moves into him slightly. Erenhart kisses her. She steps back.)* Um ... um ... *(Pause.)* I didn't ... I should of ... I have a boyfriend ... *(Pause.)*

ERENHART. I'm sorry.

LILIAN. No, I feel so stupid ... um — *(Guard enters.)*

GUARD. You're throwing things off.

LILIAN. What?

GUARD. You're throwing things off the side.

ERENHART. We're not.

DIAMOND. *(Off.)* Oh boy are you in trouble, you're gonna get it ... *(Rose comes racing around the corner, laughing, and bumps into Guard. Diamond follows her.)*

ROSE. Oops ... *(To Lilian.)* We threw nickels off the side! If we hit somebody it would go *right through their head!*

DIAMOND. *(Panting heavily.)* She's got a lot of energy, huh? Wonderful thing.

GUARD. Everybody has to go back down.

ROSE. Huh?

DIAMOND. What's the problem, pally?

GUARD. I told you, there can't be any trouble.

DIAMOND. All right now, hold on ...

GUARD. Because I will lose my job and what do I tell them —

DIAMOND. Pally, pally, we made an arrangement —

GUARD. I said to you —

DIAMOND. Okay. Shh. Okay. We're just people. That's all. We're only people. Do we need to have a fight? *(Pause.)*

GUARD. No.

DIAMOND. Of course not. Where are you from?

GUARD. India.

DIAMOND. India. Geez. Long way from home.

GUARD. This is my home. This is where I have to live.

DIAMOND. Right. Okay. *(Pause.)* Ladies. Is it me, or we looking like a buncha rubes on this thing. I mean this is for tourists.

ROSE. Let's get *out* of here.

DIAMOND. Where should we go.

ROSE. Someplace ... *elegant.* *(To Lilian.)* Don't you think?

LILIAN. I don't know.

ERENHART. Maybe you'd like to go home.

LILIAN.   Maybe I should, it's getting late ...

ERENHART.   I'll put you in a cab. *(Pause.)*

LILIAN.   Oh, I don't care where we go, I just want to get out of this *wind.*

ERENHART.   That's what we'll do. *(He indicates the way. Lilian starts out. Rose slips her arm under Lilian's and whispers to her.)*

ROSE.   Lilian. Lilian.

LILIAN.   What.

ROSE.   We're the only ones in the whole city this is happening to. Don't you think that's exciting? *(They exit. Erenhart looks toward Diamond.)*

DIAMOND.   Okay?

ERENHART.   Yes.

DIAMOND.   Aaron. It's a crime to enjoy yourself? *(Pause.)*

ERENHART.   No.

DIAMOND.   Good for you. Gimme a sec. *(Erenhart goes inside. To Guard.)* Pally. Some free advice. These ain't the pyramids. You wanna get ahead in this town? Be nice to people who pay you. *(He exits. Guard watches him go.)*

SCENE TWELVE

Back room of pinball arcade. Sound of pinball machines from other room. Fredric in chair. Mr. Barry, Art (Stranger from Scene One) staring at him. Silence. Mr. Barry yawns hugely.

BARRY.   I am *tired.*

ART.   You look tired.

BARRY.   What's the time?

ART.   *(To Fredric.)* You know the time? *(Fredric looks at his watch.)*

FREDRIC.   Twenty after twelve. *(Pause.)*

ART.   Early.

BARRY.   I was up at six.

ART. What for.

BARRY. They're digging up my street all this week.

ART. Complain.

BARRY. That gets you nowhere. If I've learned *one* thing. *(To Fredric.)* Could I just see your, on the wrist? *(Fredric moves wrist forward.)* Hunh. Nice watch. Very sporty.

FREDRIC. Thanks.

BARRY. You are welcome. *(Pause.)* Now have you noticed *that.*

FREDRIC. What.

BARRY. This current, you say "thank you" to someone, you say "excuse me," and they go, "uh-huh." Not "you're welcome." Not, ah ...

ART. "Don't mention it."

BARRY. "That's quite all all *right* ... my good ... *chap,*" whatever. Just ... "uh-huh." *(Pause.)*

FREDRIC. I haven't noticed that.

BARRY. Then it's me. *I'm* too sensitive. Thing about this city, wake up, beautiful day, feeling good, step outside, somebody dumps his little load a misery on you, you take it to someone *else,* and around it goes. That'll wear you down. Oh yeah. *(Pause.)*

FREDRIC. Once I —

ART. Hey.

FREDRIC. What.

ART. Shut up.

BARRY. Art, please. That type of talk, no. *(Pause.)* Now we had to go looking for you.

FREDRIC. I'm sorry.

BARRY. I had to send Art here out in the middle of a working day. He tells me you were rude —

FREDRIC. I didn't know who he was —

BARRY. Whatever the reason. It's not the point. *You* had the obligation. You see?

FREDRIC. Yes.

BARRY. *You* made the commitment. *You* said this and this for a certain day. That day comes, I don't see you, how am I made to feel? *(He holds up money in his hand.)* And this is not the vigorish. It's late, I search for you in the streets, and it's not even the vigorish.

ART. He was standing around.

BARRY. Mmm-hmm.

ART. Hanging on the mailbox like there's nothing better to do.

FREDRIC. I was looking for work.

ART. Checking out asses.

BARRY. Art. Now I've already mentioned.

FREDRIC. I was ... let go. Last month. My income ... has dropped. *(Pause.)*

BARRY. Mmm-hmm.

FREDRIC. I'm having a hard ... Mr. Barry? I been working since I was sixteen. Which is how I'm brought up. Okay. My father, whatever he had to, my grandfather, the day he got off the boat, lifting, digging, sweeping, all over the city, that's what I learned. Take care of myself. I'm not these people you see all over looking for handouts.

BARRY. They bother you.

FREDRIC. Mr. Barry, honestly they, they disgust me, I want to tell you this, I'm *sick* of them, acting like somebody owes them something 'cause of their own problems, things they done to themselves, *their* lives, and they go, "government owes me, rich people owe me, cause *I'm* not responsible, you know, for what's happened to *me.*" Those people, they, um, uh ...

BARRY. You're nervous.

FREDRIC. I just want you to know I'm not someone who would, would —

BARRY. It's all right. Calm down.

FREDRIC. Sorry.

BARRY. No no, seriously. Please. You're not breathing. Take a breath.

FREDRIC. Okay.

BARRY. Everybody gets a little behind. Not the end of the world. This is all that's happened to you.

FREDRIC. That's what happened.

BARRY. All right. We'll work something out. Yes? *(Fredric nods. Pause.)* Good. Good. Now. What is going on with your eyes.

FREDRIC. My ... nothing.

BARRY. You're not having a problem with your eyes.

FREDRIC. No. *(Pause.)*

BARRY. I ask because as you were speaking, they were almost vibrating.

FREDRIC. Huh.

BARRY. And the uh ...

ART. Holes.

BARRY. ... pupils, they're very small. Did you know that?

FREDRIC. No. *(Pause.)*

BARRY. Are you messing with that shit?

FREDRIC. What shit?

BARRY. That shit these people are messing with.

FREDRIC. No.

BARRY. Because it is tearing the heart right out of this town.

ART. Line them up and shoot them dead.

BARRY. What would that do.

ART. Clean the place out.

BARRY. The way we speak today, it actually frightens me.

FREDRIC. I don't go near that stuff.

BARRY. Glad to hear it. I mean what you spend the loan on, that's your affair.

FREDRIC. My rent ... I had bills due ...

BARRY. The necessities, of course. You don't want to be out in the street.

FREDRIC. No.

BARRY. But I'm going to ask you the same question, and this time please answer truthfully.

FREDRIC. I'm being truthful.

BARRY. Art. *(Art steps over to Fredric and starts going through his pockets.)* I mean it's foolish to go through this ... *(Art produces a book of matches and a small empty envelope. He shows them to Barry.)* You see now? You see where we are?

FREDRIC. It's matches ... and ... that's a pay envelope. Mr. Barry. That's what it is. *(Barry opens envelope and sniffs inside.*

59

Pause.)

BARRY.   Well. I've made a mistake.

FREDRIC.   I told you.

BARRY.   No, it's my bad judgment. I don't blame you. You have no choice, am I right? That's how it is with this junk. *(To Art.)* I paid for this. *This* is where my money went. *(He tosses the envelope aside.)*

FREDRIC.   Mr. Barry, I'm not a ... only once or twice.

BARRY.   What does that mean.

FREDRIC.   Just to relax. For a minute.

BARRY.   Like a drink. Hard day now and then, a little drink, I understand.

FREDRIC.   That's all it is.

BARRY.   So you have hard days?

FREDRIC.   Sometimes. Lately maybe.

BARRY.   You're an orphan?

FREDRIC.   Huh? No, my mother's still —

BARRY.   You're crippled? You can't find a girl? Help me understand. What's so hard about your life?

FREDRIC.   I need a *job*. I need to *do* something —

BARRY.   Last month there was a smell outside my building, did I tell you this?

FREDRIC.   No —

BARRY.   Nobody could find out what it was, they're yelling at the super, finally police come, firemen come, health department pull up the sidewalk grating, there's a woman's body inside, next to the steam pipe. She'd been living there, who knows how long. Her body, it's huge, it's wedged between the bricks, they can't budge her.

ART.   I love this kinda stuff.

BARRY.   They lower a cable off a fire engine tie it around. She's stuck tight. Now there's a crowd. Cop finds a can of motor oil, pours it down there, yank the cable and here comes this naked body. Rising up from the ground big as a boiler, and with all this oil she slips out of the cable. Crowd jumps back. Body rolls down the middle of the street. Cops argue with the firemen, firemen argue with the health inspectors. Nobody wants to touch this ... thing. Finally the super

60

brings out a hand truck, loads her on, wheels her to the wagon. When I come home he's hosing the sidewalk ... *(Pause.)* And that was that. Now tell me. This woman's life. Down in a hole. What could that have been like?

FREDRIC.   I don't know.

BARRY.   You can't figure how a person ends up that way.

FREDRIC.   No.

BARRY.   You don't know what's *hard,* do you. So many people around, and you didn't pay attention. Isn't this true? *(Pause.)*

FREDRIC.   I'm going to give it back. I had a few rough weeks but now I got things lined up. I'm going to get training ... a repairman, or a chauffeur —

BARRY.   Oh ho.

FREDRIC.   Yeah.

BARRY.   You want to be my chauffeur? Drive me around?

FREDRIC.   I'd love to, yes —

BARRY.   Could you handle a car in the city?

FREDRIC.   I could manage it —

BARRY.   You think I would hire you? Hmm? *(Pause.)*

FREDRIC.   I —

BARRY.   You think I would hire some deadbeat lying dope fiend who can't pay his *debts* because I feel *sorry* for him? You think I'm your *friend?* Do you think we have *any kind of connection?* HUH? *(He cracks Fredric repeatedly across the face.)* YOU ARE ON YOUR WAY *DOWN.* YOU STINK OF IT. YOU COME IN HERE FLOATING ON THIS SHIT EMPTY-HANDED AND YOU EXPECT *MAGIC* WILL HAPPEN? IS THIS *PARADISE?* WHERE IS YOUR SENSE? WHY DO YOU MAKE ME DO THIS? *(He grabs Fredric's wrist. Of watch.)* Look at this. This is new. Look what he buys and he can't pay me back. This is mine. It belongs to me. *(He tears the watch off Fredric's wrist and pockets it. He stands by doorway and looks into main room. Pause. To Art.)* We'll shut the doors in fifteen minutes.

ART.   Right.

FREDRIC.   I want to work ...

BARRY.   Nothing crowd tonight, close early.

ART. Okay.

FREDRIC. I want to work, Mr. Barry ... I'm trying to ... please give me a chance ...

BARRY. Now tears.

FREDRIC. I'll show you ... I can work hard ... I know the city ... there's a lot of things I can do ... just give me a chance to find something and I'll pay you back. There's work for me. I'll find something, I know I will. And next time I see you —

BARRY. *Next* time.

FREDRIC. Yes.

BARRY. *(To Art.)* See in the paper today?

ART. No.

BARRY. Guy going around town, says he's Prince of Java, his people are starving, so he raises thousands of dollars, what do you think?

ART. He's not the Prince.

BARRY. No, he's just some guy. *(He looks at Fredric again, and exits. Silence.)*

ART. Nose on the grindstone, baby. That's your little story. *(Pause.)* I'm *talking* to you. *(Fredric looks at him.)* You wanna work?

FREDRIC. What?

ART. Do ... you ... want ... to ... work.

FREDRIC. What —

ART. Yes I do no I don't.

FREDRIC. Yes ...

ART. I know a guy something you can do.

FREDRIC. What is it.

ART. You get paid, you give me ... a third. Mr. Barry doesn't know.

FREDRIC. What is it.

ART. It's *work*. Okay?

FREDRIC. 'kay. *(Pause.)*

ART. Hey. What's this? *(He lifts his shirt and twists around. A quarter-sized purplish spot is visible on his lower back.)*

FREDRIC. A spot.

ART. Got a spot there, huh?

FREDRIC.   Yeah.

ART.   It's nothing, right?

FREDRIC.   Doesn't look it.

ART.   So I got a spot. Big deal. It's nothing. Nobody knows what they're talking about.

FREDRIC.   No. *(Art lowers his shirt and turns back. Pause.)*

ART.   Wipe your face. *(Fredric starts wiping his eyes with his hand.)* Here, it's clean. *(He holds out a handkerchief.)*

SCENE THIRTEEN

An apartment. Lilian and Erenhart sitting on sofa. Rose and Diamond dancing in middle of room. Mid-tempo instrumental music playing on radio.

DIAMOND.   Did I say I was a ballroom champion?

ROSE.   You never did.

DIAMOND.   Citywide competition. Practiced three hours a day. A delivery boy then, what else did I have to do? Beat the Latins ... beat the schvartzes ... won free lunch for a year at Hellerman's. Before that I was *skinny*.

ROSE.   You're not so fat.

DIAMOND.   I stretch when I wake up. You think it's working?

LILIAN.   *(Of apartment.)* What a nice little place ...

DIAMOND.   This is just my, whatever the thing.

ERENHART.   *Pied a terre.*

ROSE.   What's that mean?

DIAMOND.   It's French. *(Singing along with music.)*
   "*I took you on a river cruise*
   That Amazon was just old news
   A thousand miles to the shore
   And not a single candy store ..."

ROSE.   *(Leaning against him.)* You have a terrible voice ...

DIAMOND.   "*We schlepped around Yosemite*
   Too much room just for you and me

63

We'll take a local, downtown bound
Warm and cozy underground ..."

ROSE.   Don't sing anymore, my brain hurts.

DIAMOND.   *"The rush, the crush*
The endless fuss
The waiting for a crosstown bus
Funny, but it's looking clear
We're crazy but we like it here ..."

I saw Billy Savine do this, a thirty piece orchestra.

ROSE.   Who's he?

DIAMOND.   Who *is* he? My God. Tell her, Lilian.

LILIAN.   I never heard of him.

ERENHART.   A famous singer.

DIAMOND.   Youth is cruel, Aaron, huh, very cruel.

ROSE.   Just dance.

DIAMOND.   They don't know. This was when this city was great. Too bad you missed it. Too bad.

ROSE.   Every time we move my head goes slosh.

DIAMOND.   Somebody's not *dancing*.

ERENHART.   We're getting orders.

LILIAN.   I only know the box step.

DIAMOND.   Nothing to be ashamed of. Aaron, stand up, take her around the room.

ERENHART.   *(To Lilian.)* I'm not very good at this.

LILIAN.   It's easy. Just watch my feet. *(She leads him in an awkward box step.)*

DIAMOND.   Here we go. This is nice. This is niceness. Look at us dancing with the pretty girls. I'm telling you I'm happy.

LILIAN.   *(Counting steps.)* One two three four ...

DIAMOND.   *(Singing.)*
"The shepherds in the Himalay ..."

ROSE.   Oh, no ...

DIAMOND.   *(Spinning Rose around.)*
"... Live forever, so they say
Lovely fellas, kind and meek
We'd die of boredom in a week
So let's keep our haunts, our little jaunts

> *Our favorite lousy restaurants*
> *Funny but it's looking —* "

(Rose suddenly goes limp and falls to the floor.) Whoa there.

LILIAN. *(Coming over.)* Rose, are you all right?

ROSE. Huh?

LILIAN. What's the matter?

ROSE. I got *dizzy*.

DIAMOND. Sure, that's all, the blood rushed out.

ROSE. There's waves in my ear ...

ERENHART. I'll get some water.

ROSE. No, I'm fine, I am. *(Pause.)* Don't everyone *look* at me. *(She gets to her feet.)* What's the time?

DIAMOND. Early, very early.

ROSE. All of a sudden I can't keep my eyes open.

LILIAN. Do you want to go home?

ROSE. Uh-uh.

DIAMOND. You just need to rest minute.

LILIAN. If you're not feeling well —

ROSE. I don't want to go home. *(To Diamond.)* Don't make me go home.

DIAMOND. Of course we won't.

ROSE. I don't have anything in my refrigerator. That's why. There's nothing *in* it.

DIAMOND. You know what, you'll lie down a little bit, you'll be fine.

ROSE. Maybe I should do that.

DIAMOND. There's a nice soft bed, just lie yourself down. Come on.

ROSE. *(To Erenhart.)* You think I'm an idiot.

ERENHART. No one thinks that.

ROSE. *(To Lilian.)* Are you my friend?

LILIAN. Rose ...

ROSE. I'm *your* friend.

LILIAN. Go lie *down*.

ROSE. I'm gonna lie down.

DIAMOND. Good for you. *(He starts leading her off.)*

ROSE. All those lights ...

DIAMOND. Uh-huh ...

ROSE. Why's everybody up so late?

DIAMOND. Hard to say.

ROSE. I know why I'm up. But why are they? What are all the other people *doing*? It doesn't make *sense* ...

DIAMOND. Who knows, sweetie, why even worry yourself ... *(Diamond and Rose exit. Pause.)*

ERENHART. I wouldn't want her head in the morning.

LILIAN. Poor Rose.

ERENHART. Does that happen often?

LILIAN. She comes into work sometimes looking like she gave all her blood. I suppose this is what.

ERENHART. You don't approve.

LILIAN. What right do I have. To say about anyone.

ERENHART. Being a criminal.

LILIAN. Shoplifter.

ERENHART. In a room with a strange man.

LILIAN. Yes. No, I mean, you're not — are you? Strange.

ERENHART. I don't know. Am I?

LILIAN. You might be. A little.

ERENHART. I think everyone's strange.

LILIAN. Not people you know.

ERENHART. Everyone.

LILIAN. People who know you.

ERENHART. Who is that? Your family? *(Pause.)*

LILIAN. No. Not anymore.

ERENHART. Friends. Rose.

LILIAN. No, she —

ERENHART. A boyfriend. A friend who's a boy. Does he know you? *(Pause. Lilian shakes her head.)* Does he know where you are tonight?

LILIAN. I don't see how.

ERENHART. Would he care?

LILIAN. Not the way you mean.

ERENHART. What way is that.

LILIAN. He ... he'd be jealous. Angry. At me. He wouldn't think about the reasons I would ... the reason why. *(Pause.)*

ERENHART. Your life needs to change.

LILIAN. Does it.

ERENHART.   You've been telling me.

LILIAN.   I never said that.

ERENHART.   What you do, where you live, who you know. All different. Did I misunderstand you? Or was that more pretending? *(Pause.)*

LILIAN.   No.

ERENHART.   Then why don't —

LILIAN.   It won't happen.

ERENHART.   Are you so sure?

LILIAN.   Can we talk about something else —

ERENHART.   Lilian. Let me help. *(Pause.)*

LILIAN.   You'll talk to my *boss*.

ERENHART.   That's not important.

LILIAN.   Would you?

ERENHART.   Yes.

LILIAN.   You'll get me a good job. With the city.

ERENHART.   I can.

LILIAN.   And an apartment.

ERENHART.   Like this?

LILIAN.   No, bigger. Bigger, higher and no rent.

ERENHART.   Is that what you want?

LILIAN.   Would you give it to me?

ERENHART.   You're joking now.

LILIAN.   Am I?

ERENHART.   I can't tell. *(Pause.)*

LILIAN.   You're married.

ERENHART.   What?

LILIAN.   Aren't you married? You are, aren't you? Why don't you *say* it. *(Pause.)*

ERENHART.   Yes.

LILIAN.   Was I not supposed to *know* that? *(Diamond enters from other room. Pause.)*

DIAMOND.   So. She's sleeping. That's a tired girl. *(He pours himself a drink.)* I thought you know, rest for couple a minutes, but uh ... she's out. Out for the count. *(Pause.)* Well. What are you gonna do. Can't always ... *(Pause.)* You two, all right, huh?

ERENHART.   Yes.

DIAMOND.   Good, good. Doing all right. *(He drinks. Pause. To Lilian.)* She was very warm, I unbuttoned the top, so if you look in, that's what. *(Pause.)* Yeah. Okay. Okay. You go on ... I'm sitting. Just gonna sit. *(He sits on sofa. Rubbing face.)* Late now, huh. All of a sudden.

ERENHART.   It creeps up.

DIAMOND.   What I used to do, I was I kid? Grab on the back of a truck, going uptown, hang on there, you wouldn't believe how quick it ended. How the city just ended. Like a magic trick. Into a field, tomatoes, a big bite and juice running down, you didn't care, it was fine. A fine thing. And sleep right there, all in the green and hot sun, that was sleep. Real sleep. Could that happen today? I don't think so. I don't think it could. Huh, Aaron. Huh.

ERENHART.   No. All gone. *(Diamond lets out a deep breath and shuts his eyes.)*

DIAMOND.   Look at me. Look what I'm doing now ... *(He sits there with eyes shut. Silence.)*

ERENHART.   "The Golden Age."

LILIAN.   What?

ERENHART.   Life was perfect. The streets were clean and nobody ever cursed. And he was there, the lucky boy who ventured forth and made good before it all went to pieces. He rams it down my throat like we had something in common.

LILIAN.   It's how he remembers.

ERENHART.   It's his excuse.

LILIAN.   Is he married too?

ERENHART.   That's not what I meant.

LILIAN.   No. Of course. *(Pause.)* I have to check on Rose.

ERENHART.   He's stealing. Hundreds of thousands. You know that, don't you? *(Pause. Lilian looks at him.)* Oh yes. Mr. Diamond who loves the city. It doesn't bother him at all.

LILIAN.   Stealing how.

ERENHART.   This project, Lilian. The amounts involved. You don't realize how much. Mr. Diamond knows. He understands how expensive a few truckloads of steel rods can turn out to be, among friends. By the time this plant is finished

... or abandoned ... or used for a bus yard just to cut losses, it could cost ... anything. That's worth celebrating.

LILIAN. You know this?

ERENHART. Very well.

LILIAN. Why don't you do something.

ERENHART. It wouldn't make any difference.

LILIAN. You keep saying that.

ERENHART. It's what I've learned. I used to worry about the poor, Lilian, the poor bothered me, I felt something had to be done. Save the city you had to save the poor. Give them air and sun and modern appliances, and, *trees*, we believed they responded well to trees and what has been discovered, what we know now at great expense is that none of that matters. Whatever you give the poor they destroy, they can't help it. They fill up jails and hospitals, they live ten to a room, they shoot each other over meaningless things. And this is what we're about now, working for the city, controlling the poor and the wild in their masses, containing them, somehow. It's all we can manage and there's no strength left for anything else. I don't have the strength.

LILIAN. So just let it happen.

ERENHART. No.

LILIAN. Something wrong and don't even try —

ERENHART. That's not the situation. *(Pause.)*

LILIAN. He's paying you.

ERENHART. Yes.

LILIAN. How much.

ERENHART. It doesn't ma —

LILIAN. How much?

ERENHART. More than my salary. This year and next.

LILIAN. And that's enough.

ERENHART. It's nothing.

LILIAN. Then why.

ERENHART. If not me ...

LILIAN. You decided.

ERENHART. ... someone else, and what would I have.

LILIAN. You *decided*.

ERENHART. Stealing a watch.

LILIAN. That's different.

ERENHART. How? Because you want to confess? Punishing yourself, Lilian. Is that the same as being honest? *(Pause.)* You see. To live this way. With so much taken out and nothing given back. My god. You don't believe in ghosts, the city's full of them. I won't be one. My decision. *(Pause.)*

LILIAN. That money.

ERENHART. Yes.

LILIAN. You'll spend it on your wife.

ERENHART. No.

LILIAN. Don't you love her.

ERENHART. We're strangers.

LILIAN. Like you said.

ERENHART. Strange, yes.

LILIAN. What will you spend it on.

ERENHART. Something that matters.

LILIAN. I thought nothing mattered. *(Pause. Erenhart steps up to her.)*

ERENHART. *(Of music on radio.)* Could you dance to this?

LILIAN. Too slow.

ERENHART. Let me try. *(He puts his arms around her. They sway slightly back and forth. A long kiss. They stop moving. He starts unbuttoning her blouse. She steps away.)*

LILIAN. I don't feel right. *(Pause.)*

ERENHART. I understand. *(Pause.)*

LILIAN. Mr. Diamond ...

ERENHART. He won't wake up.

LILIAN. No, that's ... *(Pause.)* I should go.

ERENHART. How will you get home?

LILIAN. I'll be fine.

ERENHART. You can't take the subway at this hour. Here's for a cab.

LILIAN. No. Thank you.

ERENHART. *(Taking out money.)* Take it. *(He holds it out.)* Take it, please. It won't poison you. *(Pause. Lilian steps over and takes money. Erenhart holds her hand.)* You dislike me that much?

LILIAN. No.

ERENHART.   Is what I've done wrong.

LILIAN.   I don't know. No. I don't know. *(Pause.)*

ERENHART.   Stay here. *(Lilian shakes her head. Pause.)* Lilian. I've been honest with you. I've spoken things. Can't you be honest with me? *(Pause.)* Here we are. *(He steps forward. They kiss.)* I'm shutting off the lights. *(He does. Square patch of window light on floor.)*

LILIAN.   Never dark. Never ever.

ERENHART.   Close your eyes.

LILIAN.   Let's take everything.

ERENHART.   Yes, shh.

LILIAN.   Whatever we see. Whatever we want. Take it.

ERENHART.   I'll give you, yes.

LILIAN.   Just decide. Why not. Why *not* ... *(He kisses her again. He slips his hand under her blouse.)* Let me think, for a minute.

ERENHART.   Shh, don't worry.

LILIAN.   I want to *think*, I have to —

ERENHART.   It's all right.

LILIAN.   No, I —

ERENHART.   *(Placing his hand over her mouth.)* Shh, shhh. Stop it. Who else understands you. Who else anywhere. That's what matters. That's the only thing ... *(He lowers her down to the floor.)* Shush. Shush, don't let them know. It's just us. Stop it. Please. You shouldn't — Stop. *(Holding her down.)* Now we're ghosts. Yes. We need to be still. That's important. Stop it. Because listen. Wait. Listen. How quiet. Did you know. Sometimes everybody takes a breath at once. *(He climbs on top of her.)* You'll see, Lilian ... you'll see ... how much better ...

SCENE FOURTEEN

Interior of abandoned building. Sound of dripping water. Fredric and group of Scabs standing about silently. Foreman enters in work gear.

FOREMAN. I don't need this many.

SCAB ONE. I was here first.

FOREMAN. I need three.

SCAB TWO. *(Of Fredric.)* He just got here.

FREDRIC. Art told me to come.

FOREMAN. Who?

FREDRIC. Art. From the pinball.

FOREMAN. Art from the pinball. *(Scab Two laughs. To Scab Three.)* Were you here last night?

SCAB THREE. That's right, chief. You know me. *(Pause.)*

FOREMAN. Okay. You three. Let's go.

FREDRIC. Wait ...

SCAB ONE. Pay's forty, right.

FOREMAN. Work first.

SCAB ONE. But it's forty?

FOREMAN. It's what it is.

FREDRIC. I'll work for thirty.

FOREMAN. You will, huh.

SCAB TWO. Get outta here.

FREDRIC. I'll work harder than him. You'll see. Hire me. *(Pause.)*

FOREMAN. Maybe tomorrow.

FREDRIC. Twenty.

SCAB TWO. Go play *pinball.*

FOREMAN. *(To the Scabs.)* Get into the walls like this. You need a crowbar. The plaster, molding, the lathe, just rip it up. Tear up the floor.

SCAB ONE. Fuck it all up.

FOREMAN. All the pipes, fixtures, doorknobs, leave them alone, somebody come by for them later. I see you take anything, whatever small, you're gone, understood? That's how it goes. *(To Scab One.)* You. Top floor, work down. Watch out for rotted joists. *(To Scab Two.)* You come with me. We'll do the basement. Cops show up, drop the tools and out. I'll catch up with you later. Any questions?

SCAB TWO.   What if we got to pee?

FOREMAN.   Don't do it on the stairs. I could slip and hurt myself and that would make me mad. *(He reaches into sack, pulls out crowbars and distributes them. One is left over. Foreman looks at Fredric.)* Twenty dollars. *(He holds out crowbar. Fredric takes it.)* With him. This floor. Pick up where you left off. Work fast. Let's go, everybody. *(Scab One goes upstairs. Foreman and Scab Two head for basement. Fredric and Scab Three watch them go.)*

SCAB THREE.   Keep an eye on him. He lights out, we don't get paid.

FREDRIC.   He gonna cheat us?

SCAB THREE.   He already cheating.

FREDRIC.   Cheated me.

SCAB THREE.   You the only person here?

FREDRIC.   No ...

SCAB THREE.   Well then. *(He starts digging into wall with crowbar. Fredric follows.)* Smell that?

FREDRIC.   What.

SCAB THREE.   Gas leak.

FREDRIC.   Should we tell him?

SCAB THREE.   What you want to say.

FREDRIC.   The gas. It could blow up.

SCAB THREE.   That's right.

FREDRIC.   He should know.

SCAB THREE.   You think he gonna call the fire department?

FREDRIC.   I don't wanna get killed in here.

SCAB THREE.   Don't hit the gas line.

FREDRIC.   Where is it?

SCAB THREE.   Find out when you hit it. *(Pause.)* Don't matter anyhow. Next month this be a big hole in the ground.

FREDRIC.   Then what're we doing.

SCAB THREE. What you think.

FREDRIC. Scabbing. *(Scab Three picks up section of pipe from nearby pile.)*

SCAB THREE. What this.

FREDRIC. Pipe.

SCAB THREE. Copper. Hundred year old maybe. Melt it down nobody know where it from. That railing brass. Steps you come up, they marble. That man smart, steal it all little piece at a time 'fore the wrecking ball. Look up. *(Pause.)* Go 'head. I ain't gonna *do* something to you. *(Fredric does so.)* See?

FREDRIC. Naked lady.

SCAB THREE. There you go.

FREDRIC. Floating on a cloud or something ...

SCAB THREE. Bunch a Indians ... them guys in black tights hopping off a boat ...

FREDRIC. Pilgrims.

SCAB THREE. Scary looking mothers.

FREDRIC. What is this place.

SCAB THREE. Where *you* from?

FREDRIC. City.

SCAB THREE. You ain't you been here.

FREDRIC. Don't remember.

SCAB THREE. Uh-*huh*. *(Pause.)* This the ballroom. Everybody dance kissing hands and shit. Big swimming pool on the roof. Train station downstairs. For the *guests*.

FREDRIC. Dj'you work here?

SCAB THREE. *Lived* here.

FREDRIC. *Right.*

SCAB THREE. Till they shut it down get rid of us.

FREDRIC. You're a millionaire, huh.

SCAB THREE. Man. Don't you know nothing? This the *Plymouth Hotel.*

FREDRIC. So?

SCAB THREE. This the worst shelter in the city. *The* worst. Two, three hundred beds right on this floor. They so close together you scratch your balls you making somebody else happy. Ten o'clock they lock the doors ain't nobody get out.

Lights off and there you be three hundred farting sneezing maniac fuckers man. No way you sleep. And there gotta be someone, he fixing you, pick you out special like he in love, come up say, "where my comb," you go "huh," "gimme me my comb from last *week* back," you don't know what the *fuck* he's talking with that shit ... (*Pause.*) And so he got a *knife*, right, and he just wanna make you ... (*Pause. He turns and begins dismantling radiator. Pause. Fredric goes to work with crowbar, swinging furiously at the wall. Scab Three pauses to watch. After several seconds Fredric stops, breathing hard. He sees Scab Three looking at him.*)

FREDRIC.   He said work fast.

SCAB THREE.   I guess you did. (*He indicates the radiator.*) This is heavy. (*Fredric comes over and helps Scab Three move radiator. As they work:*)

FREDRIC.   You live in the street?

SCAB THREE.   Squat. Over by Franklin Park. They six of us. Water pipe in the basement. An I hook up lectricity from the cable.

FREDRIC.   How'd you do that?

SCAB THREE.   Lectricity, plumbing, that's what I *know*. Worked construction nine years. All them offices going up. That was fine money. They tell you where it went?

FREDRIC.   Uh-uh.

SCAB THREE.   Nobody told me neither. (*Pause.*) Ever been on fire?

FREDRIC.   No ...

SCAB THREE.   Think it's funny?

FREDRIC.   No. (*Scab Three holds out arm and rolls up sleeve to reveal thick scar.*)

SCAB THREE.   I was laughing. All on fire an laughing. Got onto that shit, right. Live for it. Do anything to get it. Lost my people. Lost everything I had. (*Pause.*)

FREDRIC.   You okay now?

SCAB THREE.   I don't know what that mean, "okay." I'm trying to be good. Be a good person. It expensive, man. Cost me something every day. (*Pause.*)

FREDRIC.   I'm Fredric.

SCAB THREE.   Uh-huh. You from around ... *Steuben* Avenue.

FREDRIC.   What?

SCAB THREE.   Ain't that where you from?

FREDRIC.   You're guessing.

SCAB THREE.   You got the accent.

FREDRIC.   Bull*shit.*

SCAB THREE.   Everybody talk a little different. *(Pause.)*

FREDRIC.   What's your name.

SCAB THREE.   Phillip.

FREDRIC.   Okay, you're from the ...

SCAB THREE.   Yeah?

FREDRIC.   You're not from here.

SCAB THREE.   You Steuben boys *dumb.*

FREDRIC.   Just hold on.

SCAB THREE.   Shit. You give me one hour I show you every place I ever been. Show you where I'm born, where I work, where I used to live. My whole life happen right here in this city. Know what that make me?

FREDRIC.   What?

SCAB THREE.   A *native.*

FREDRIC.   So? I am too.

SCAB THREE.   Ah, you dreaming, friend.

FREDRIC.   Steuben Avenue.

SCAB THREE.   Maybe that the city, man. But it ain't *in* the city. And you *know* that's true. So you show me some respect.

FREDRIC.   *(Returning to wall with crowbar.)* Kiss my ass.

SCAB THREE.   You wishing. *(As Fredric swings crowbar into wall.)* Don't touch that.

FREDRIC.   Why not.

SCAB THREE.   Gas line. *(Pause.)*

FREDRIC.   Okay. *(Scab Three nods. He ties a rag around the pipe to mark it. Pause.)*

SCAB THREE.   What you doing here, Fredric.

FREDRIC.   Huh?

SCAB THREE.   Ain't ragging on you but ... you don't know shit.

FREDRIC.   I take care of myself. That's what I'm doing. *(Pause.)*

SCAB THREE.   Looking at trouble?

FREDRIC.   I'm, looking. Yeah. *(Pause.)* I can't ... keep up, you know? Everything else shooting up ninety stories on top a me, all of a sudden I'm underground. Man I want to breathe. I need to breathe for a second. Why can't I fucking breathe ...

SCAB THREE.   Relax man. Do the work.

FREDRIC.   Yeah. *(Pause.)* Phillip. You got anything?

SCAB THREE.   Uh-uh. Told you.

FREDRIC.   Just a taste see me through?

SCAB THREE.   You on your own with that.

FREDRIC.   No, see then I can work, so —

SCAB THREE.   Step outside find someone five minutes make you happy. *(Pause.)*

FREDRIC.   Phillip. Lend me some money. *(Scab Three laughs.)* Come on. I'll pay you back soon as he —

SCAB THREE.   You don't know who you talking to.

FREDRIC.   Come on man, something. You were here last night. You got paid. What you do with the money?

SCAB THREE.   That ain't your business.

FREDRIC.   Five dollars.

SCAB THREE.   Ain't gonna happen.

FREDRIC.   No. You can. Five dollars. So I can work. Give me something.

SCAB THREE.   Get away, man.

FREDRIC.   Help me. I just need to get through it, then I can — help me out. Please. *(Pause.)* Phillip. Help me, *goddamit.* I NEED SOME FUCKING AIR. *(Pause.)*

SCAB THREE.   Yeah well ... next time. *(Pause.)* You in my *way. (Fredric steps back. Scab Three returns to work. Fredric steps up to gas line. With a shout he lifts the crowbar and swings it at the line. Scab Three wheels around and grabs Fredric's arm, holding it.)* You wanna *die,* man? Huh? Get outta here. Cut your fucking wrists. Go hump the third rail you got the balls. But get the fuck away from me. I got a hundred ways go missing every day and I ain't asked you for no help tonight. You hear? DO YOU HEAR ME? *(He grabs Fredric's crowbar and tosses it away.)* Get *out.* Get the fuck out. Selfish *motherfucker. (He pushes*

Fredric away. Fredric stumbles, walks a few steps, then stops. Scab Three keeps looking at him.) What you waiting for. Get done with yourself. Go on. *(Fredric stands there. Scab Three steps forward. Foreman enters with sack of pipe fittings.)*

FOREMAN. Hey. Hey. Screwing around here? Wrong place for that.

SCAB THREE. Just catching our breath, chief.

FOREMAN. Save that for later. Come on. I'm watching you. Outta here by seven. *(He exits. Fredric picks up his crowbar. Scab Three watches him. Pause.)*

FREDRIC. That part.

SCAB THREE. What.

FREDRIC. Of the wall, is it safe? *(Pause.)*

SCAB THREE. Look okay. *(Fredric walks up to wall, takes a breath and starts working. Scab Three watches him for several seconds. Then he returns to work as well. They tear at the wall in silence.)* This is work.

FREDRIC. Right.

SCAB THREE. Gonna get *paid*.

FREDRIC. Counting on it. *(Pause.)*

SCAB THREE. Stupid, Fredric.

FREDRIC. Yeah.

SCAB THREE. Stupid shit. *(They work. Silence. Of plaster.)* Get all over you.

FREDRIC. I don't mind.

SCAB THREE. All right then. This town ain't killed us yet. *(They work.)*

SCENE FIFTEEN

Department store. Rose behind counter, holding her head. Three tones sound. Lilian enters hurriedly, wearing different clothing. Rose glances at her.

LILIAN. I know.

ROSE. Did I say anything?

LILIAN. I couldn't help it. *(Pause.)* Rose. All right? *(Pause.)*

ROSE.   Kraus came by.

LILIAN.   When?

ROSE.   Five, six minutes.

LILIAN.   The train —

ROSE.   Uh-huh. *(Pause.)*

LILIAN.   Look, I'm sorry.

ROSE.   About what.

LILIAN.   That I left. I had to leave.

ROSE.   I guess you did.

LILIAN.   You were asleep and ...

ROSE.   You left me there. *(Pause.)*

LILIAN.   What happened?

ROSE.   Nothing.

LILIAN.   When you woke up?

ROSE.   I didn't wake up. I'm not waking up today. *(Pause.)*

LILIAN.   Was he there?

ROSE.   Who.

LILIAN.   Mister, Mister ... my god. I don't know his last name.

ROSE.   Didn't you go together.

LILIAN.   No.

ROSE.   Well I didn't see him. *(Pause.)* Why'd you leave.

LILIAN.   I just wanted to. We talked for a little and ... I just wanted to go home. That's all. I couldn't wake you up. *(Pause.)*

ROSE.   So I was really out of it.

LILIAN.   You really were.

ROSE.   How about that.

LILIAN.   Yeah. *(Pause.)*

ROSE.   Mr. Diamond was there.

LILIAN.   Uh-huh.

ROSE.   He was there all right. *(Pause.)* He couldn't do anything, you know.

LILIAN.   What do you mean.

ROSE.   I mean he tried and he couldn't. He wasn't able to. It was kind of strange. *(Pause.)* Made me breakfast.

LILIAN.   Did he.

ROSE.   Yeah. He likes to cook. Not the first thing you think with him. Eggs and cream something, it was very good. All right listen, he wants to take me to the theater?

LILIAN. Really.

ROSE. Anything I want to see.

LILIAN. *Happy Go Lucky.*

ROSE. That's old now.

LILIAN. Then something else.

ROSE. I feel like shit. This is actually true. *(Pause.)* Here. I forgot. *(She produces a small wrapped box from beneath counter.)*

LILIAN. What's that.

ROSE. I don't know. It came for you. Guy wanted a *tip*, believe that. *(Pause.)* Aren't you gonna open it? *(Lilian looks at box. Fredric enters.)* Oh lovely. Here comes another one ... *(He comes up to counter.)* Can I help you? *(Fredric looks at Lilian.)* Can I *help* you? *(Recognizing him.)* Oh, you're —

FREDRIC. *(To Lilian.)* I need to talk to you.

LILIAN. What are you doing here.

FREDRIC. Can we please.

LILIAN. I'm working now.

FREDRIC. You walked away from me.

LILIAN. That's how you remember it?

FREDRIC. I called you after. You weren't — where were you.

LILIAN. What do you care.

FREDRIC. I'm just asking.

LILIAN. It's not your business.

FREDRIC. Why not? *(Pause.)* Why the fuck not?

ROSE. I'm sneaking a cigarette.

LILIAN. Rose. Wait. Wait. *(Rose exits. Pause.)*

FREDRIC. All alone.

LILIAN. Don't make trouble here.

FREDRIC. I'll do what I want.

LILIAN. There's guards.

FREDRIC. You better be afraid.

LILIAN. I can call them. I'll do it. *(Pause.)*

FREDRIC. *(Looking at watch display.)* That's like the one.

LILIAN. What.

FREDRIC. You gave me.

LILIAN. Yes. *(Pause.)*

FREDRIC. I'm sorry.

LILIAN. For what.

FREDRIC. How I acted. *(Pause.)*

LILIAN. You don't treat me right.

FREDRIC. I know.

LILIAN. Like someone you don't care about.

FREDRIC. I care about you.

LILIAN. I don't think so.

FREDRIC. I love you. *(Pause.)* I need you.

LILIAN. You need me.

FREDRIC. I want to take care of you. I want to try. Last night was bad. For me. Can't I apologize. Can't I ... try and change. I know I can change. Please. Let me show you. I know I can be better. Let me try. *(Pause. Lilian moves forward. She places her hands on the counter. Fredric clasps her hands and lowers his forehead against her palms. Pause.)*

LILIAN. Do you have it?

FREDRIC. What.

LILIAN. The watch.

FREDRIC. Not here.

LILIAN. Where is it?

FREDRIC. You gave it to me.

LILIAN. I need it back.

FREDRIC. You said —

LILIAN. I want it back.

FREDRIC. Would you listen to me.

LILIAN. What did you do with it?

FREDRIC. I don't want to talk about —

LILIAN. You don't have it. Do you. You don't.

FREDRIC. No.

LILIAN. What did, you lost it? *(Pause.)* You sold it. Is that what you did?

FREDRIC. I'm trying to *say* something.

LILIAN. You love me.

FREDRIC. Yes.

LILIAN. I can't *hear* this now.

FREDRIC.   Just promise you'll —

LILIAN.   Can't you see what you look like?

FREDRIC.   I've been working. I worked all night.

LILIAN.   Doing what? *(Pause.)* What were you doing?

FREDRIC.   I got *paid,* all right.

LILIAN.   No. It's not all right. Where were you? Where were you for me? *(Pause.)* My god. Look at you. You're filthy. There's people on the street you cross to get away from.

FREDRIC.   That's not what I am.

LILIAN.   You don't *know* what you are.

FREDRIC.   Give me a chance —

LILIAN.   "Take *care* of me." You can't even take care of yourself.

FREDRIC.   Lily. Please. I'm here, okay, don't, treat me like a ghost —

LILIAN.   *I can't be around you.* Don't you see that? I don't want to *live* that way. You can't help me. You scare me. It scares me to look at you. *(Rose enters quickly.)*

ROSE.   He's coming. Do I smell of smoke? *(Kraus enters and stands behind Fredric.)*

KRAUS.   Everything all right, ladies?

ROSE.   Yes, Mr. Kraus.

KRAUS.   Lilian.

LILIAN.   Morning Mr. Kraus.

KRAUS.   When you're done with this gentleman.

LILIAN.   He's done now.

FREDRIC.   No I'm not.

LILIAN.   He doesn't want to buy anything.

KRAUS.   What are you looking for, sir. *(Pause.)* Sir? What can I help you find.

FREDRIC.   Nothing.

KRAUS.   Nothing I can help you with.

FREDRIC.   That's *correct. (Pause.)*

KRAUS.   You don't need help finding the exit.

FREDRIC.   What?

KRAUS.   The exit to the store.

FREDRIC.   No. I'm talking to … *(Pause.)* I'm not a … she knows me. I'm her boyfriend. She *knows* me. *(To Lilian.)* Tell

him. Tell him who I am. *(Kraus looks at Lilian. She looks away.)*
KRAUS.   Sir. *(Pause.)*
FREDRIC.   Ask her where she was last night. That's what she doesn't —
KRAUS.   Take your problems outside.
FREDRIC.   I don't have problems. Keep away. *(To Lilian.)* Tell him.
KRAUS.   That's enough, sir.
FREDRIC.   *(To Lilian.)* Is that how you want it? *(Pause.)* Why don't you *answer* me.
LILIAN.   I don't know you. *(To the others.)* I don't know who he is. *(Pause.)* Leave me alone. That's what I want. *(Pause.)*
FREDRIC.   You think you're *special*. Don't you.
KRAUS.   Mister. You're done. As of now. If you're looking for trouble we'll give you trouble. All right?
FREDRIC.   What's so special ... about *you*. *(He exits.)*
KRAUS.   There's no end to them.
ROSE.   No.
KRAUS.   Three asleep in the entrance this morning. You're afraid to step through the door. This is not my job. Doing this.
ROSE.   He's always coming in. He's nuts.
KRAUS.   And you get tired of feeling sorry.
ROSE.   What can you do. *(Pause.)* I read in the paper about a person who —
KRAUS.   Lilian.
LILIAN.   Yes ...
KRAUS.   How long have you worked for us.
LILIAN.   What? Uh ... eight months ...
KRAUS.   Are you happy here.
LILIAN.   Yes.
KRAUS.   I wonder if you are. From what I've been told. Am I right to wonder that? *(Pause. He holds out a slip of pink paper.)* Do you know what this is? *(Pause.)* Yesterday —
ROSE.   It's wasn't her, Mr. Kraus.
LILIAN.   Rose —
ROSE.   The other girl made a mistake, she's afraid to —
LILIAN.   Please. Rose. Don't. *(Pause.)* Mr. Kraus. I want to

83

explain. I want you to know what happened.

KRAUS. Yes? *(Pause.)*

LILIAN. The watch was on the counter. There was no one around. I don't know why. I don't have a reason. I ... *(Pause.)* I forgot about it. That I left it there. *(Pause.)* The crazy man. Who always comes in. He took it. He stole it. I didn't tell anyone because ... it was my fault. *(Pause.)*

KRAUS. Stolen.

LILIAN. Yes. I'm to blame. I did it. *(Pause.)*

KRAUS. *(Placing pink slip on counter.)* Fill this out.

LILIAN. What?

KRAUS. Just fill it out. *(Pause.)* A problem with the *register.* You need an adjustment form.

LILIAN. That's not —

KRAUS. It doesn't matter.

LILIAN. The crazy man —

KRAUS. It doesn't *matter.* It's too late now. Fill this out so there's something for upstairs. *(He signs bottom of paper.)* Fill it out, put it under the drawer. Pay more attention.

LILIAN. I'm sorry.

KRAUS. After eight months? Don't leave things on the counter. Think about me a little. Please.

LILIAN. I will, I promise.

ROSE. I'll keep an eye on her, Mr. Kraus.

KRAUS. *(Glancing around the store.)* Are we getting any customers at all? *(He exits. Pause.)*

ROSE. Okay? *(Lilian nods.)* Told you, didn't I.

LILIAN. He said fill this out ...

ROSE. As long as you're careful?

LILIAN. Yesterday's date ...

ROSE. You can just do what you want.

LILIAN. The amount ...

ROSE. And lying to his face?

LILIAN. How much was it ...

ROSE. Very slick. I can't *believe* that was you.

LILIAN. I'm trying to concentrate ...

ROSE. All *right.* *(Pause.)* I'm your friend, you know. *(Pause.)*

LILIAN. I know.

ROSE.   You don't like me but I'm your friend.

LILIAN.   I like you.

ROSE.   Oh go to hell.

LILIAN.   I do, Rose. I really do. I ... *(Pause.)* Thank you. *(Pause.)*

ROSE.   *(Of package.)* Aren't you gonna open that? *(Pause. Lilian tears off the wrapping. revealing a fancy gift box. She opens notecard and reads it.)* Well. Who's in love with you?

LILIAN.   No one.

ROSE.   You *have* to tell me. *(She tears up the card.)* You can't do that. It's not fair. *Lilian* ... *(Pause.)* I know who it is anyway.

LILIAN.   Do you.

ROSE.   I saw you kiss him last night. *(Pause.)* Don't be so embarrassed. He was very nice. *(Pause.)* *I* thought he was nice.

LILIAN.   A nice man.

ROSE.   Then what's the problem?

LILIAN.   No problem. *(Pause.)*

ROSE.   Aren't you even gonna see what it is?

LILIAN.   You go ahead. *(Rose opens the box.)*

ROSE.   Well look at that. That's ... beautiful. *(She takes out the contents.)* A little chocolate city. Oh you have to see. Bridges and buses and everything. Right in front of you. *(Pause.)* Lilian.

LILIAN.   What.

ROSE.   We could eat up the whole place in two big bites, and no one could stop us. *(Laughing.)* That'd show em, huh?

LILIAN.   Yes. Wouldn't it be nice.

END

PROPERTY LIST

Man's watch (CUSTOMER)
Newspaper (FREDRIC)
Metallic pieces of junk (WOMAN WITH JUNK)
Cigarette (WAITER ONE)
Drinks (ROSE, LILLIAN)
Bucket of champagne (YOUNG WAITER)
4 champagne glasses (YOUNG WAITER)
Pair of pants (MAN WITH PANTS)
Money (bills) (BILL, FREDRIC, DIAMOND, ERENHART,
    BARRY)
Book of matches (FREDRIC)
1 small, empty envelope (FREDRIC)
Handkerchief (ART)
Sack (FOREMAN) with:
    4 crowbars
    pipe fittings
Battered canteen (SCAB THREE)
Small wrapped box (ROSE) with:
    city made of chocolate
Pink office form (KRAUS)

SOUND EFFECTS

3 tones
Door lock buzzer
Subway train sounds
Electric bell ringing
Pinball machines sounds
Mid-tempo instrumental music
Dripping water

NEW PLAYS

• **A QUESTION OF MERCY by David Rabe.** The Obie Award-winning playwright probes the sensitive and controversial issue of doctor-assisted suicide in the age of AIDS in this poignant drama. *"There are many devastating ironies in Mr. Rabe's beautifully considered, piercingly clear-eyed work ... " –The NY Times. "With unsettling candor and disturbing insight, the play arouses pity and understanding of a troubling subject ... Rabe's provocative tale is an affirmation of dignity that rings clear and true." –Variety.* [6M, 1W] ISBN: 0-8222-1643-4

• **A DOLL'S HOUSE by Henrik Ibsen, adapted by Frank McGuinness. Winner of the 1997 Tony Award for best revival.** *"New, raw, gut-twisting and gripping. Easily the hottest drama this season." –USA Today. "Bold, brilliant and alive." –The Wall Street Journal. "A thunderclap of an evening that takes your breath away." –Time. "The stuff of Broadway legend." –Associated Press.* [4M, 4W, 2 boys] ISBN: 0-8222-1636-1

• **THE WAITING ROOM by Lisa Loomer.** Three women from different centuries meet in a doctor's waiting room in this dark comedy about the timeless quest for beauty -- and its cost. *" ... THE WAITING ROOM ... is a bold, risky melange of conflicting elements that is ... terrifically moving ... There's no resisting the fierce emotional pull of the play." – The NY Times. " ... one of the high points of this year's Off-Broadway season ... THE WAITING ROOM is well worth a visit." –Back Stage.* [7M, 4W, flexible casting] ISBN: 0-8222-1594-2

• **MR. PETERS' CONNECTIONS by Arthur Miller.** Mr. Miller describes the protagonist as existing in a dream-like state when the mind is "freed to roam from real memories to conjectures, from trivialities to tragic insights, from terror of death to glorying in one's being alive." With this memory play, the Tony Award and Pulitzer Prize-winner reaffirms his stature as the world's foremost dramatist. *" ... a cross between Joycean stream-of-consciousness and Strindberg's dream plays, sweetened with a dose of William Saroyan's philosophical whimsy ... CONNECTIONS is most intriguing ... Miller scholars will surely find many connections of their own to make between this work and the author's earlier plays." –The NY Times.* [5M, 3W] ISBN: 0-8222-1687-6

• **THE STEWARD OF CHRISTENDOM by Sebastian Barry.** A freely imagined portrait of the author's great-grandfather, the last Chief Superintendent of the Dublin Metropolitan Police. *"MAGNIFICENT ... the cool, elegiac eye of James Joyce's THE DEAD; the bleak absurdity of Samuel Beckett's lost, primal characters; the cosmic anger of KING LEAR ..." –The NY Times. "Sebastian Barry's compassionate imaging of an ancestor he never knew is among the most poignant onstage displays of humanity in recent memory." –Variety.* [5M, 4W] ISBN: 0-8222-1609-4

• **SYMPATHETIC MAGIC by Lanford Wilson. Winner of the 1997 Obie for best play.** The mysteries of the universe, and of human and artistic creation, are explored in this award-winning play. *"Lanford Wilson's idiosyncratic SYMPATHETIC MAGIC is his BEST PLAY YET ... the rare play you WANT ... chock-full of ideas, incidents, witty or poetic lines, scientific and philosophical argument ... you'll find your intellectual faculties racing." – New York Magazine. "The script is like a fully notated score, next to which most new plays are cursory lead sheets." –The Village Voice.* [5M, 3W] ISBN: 0-8222-1630-2

DRAMATISTS PLAY SERVICE, INC.
440 Park Avenue South, New York, NY 10016 212-683-8960 Fax 212-213-1539
postmaster@dramatists.com www.dramatists.com